F A N T A S Y
CHOCOLATE
D E S S E R T S

**Mexican
Chocolate
Custard Cake,
page 62**

By Robert Lambert

*Photography
By Patricia Brabant*

Copyright © 1988 by Robert Lambert

Produced by EGOZINE Productions, San Anselmo, California

Art direction, photographic and food styling by Robert Lambert

Book design and production by Laura Lamar of MAX

Editing by Carey Charlesworth

Photography assistance by Laurie Thomas and Edy Owen

Keyboarding by David Van Ness and Hal Lewis; formatting on Macintosh SE in Ready,Set,Go! 4.0a by Changhwan Kim of MAX
Typographic output by Krishna Copy, San Francisco
Printed in Japan by Toppan Printing Company, Tokyo

Library of Congress Cataloging-in-Publication Data

Lambert, Robert, 1948–
Fantasy chocolate desserts/by Robert Lambert; photography by Patricia Brabant. p. cm.

Includes indexes.
ISBN 0-87701-555-4
ISBN 0-87701-541-4 (pbk.)
1. Cookery (Chocolate) 2. Desserts. I. Brabant, Patricia. II. Title.
TX767.C5L26 1988
641.6'374—dc19
88-22807CIP

Distributed in Canada by
Raincoast Books
112 East Third Avenue
Vancouver, British Columbia V5T 1C8

10 9 8 7 6 5 4 3 2 1

Chronicle Books
275 Fifth Street
San Francisco, California 94103

Cover: Chevron Strawberries, page 60

Acknowledgements

This book is the result of the culinary collaboration and spiritual support of many friends and colleagues. I especially wish to thank: ● John Basgall for years of support and patient listening. ● John Baylin, who first inspired me to write books, then inspired me to cook. ● Patricia Brabant, who had the confidence in me to begin this book 6 years ago . . . a collaborator made in heaven. ● Carey Charlesworth, whose painstaking editing brought out the best in me. ● Edible Art of San Francisco, especially its founders Sharon Polster and Robin McMillian and present owner Meme Pederson, for providing me with the opportunities to do my very best. ● Tom Hart for encouragement and support. ● Greg Jeresek for his love and support. ● Laura Lamar for her selfless dedication to designing my fantasy in black and white. ● Donna Lazarus for her black and white squiggle plate. ● Amy Nathan, mentor and friend. ● David Rubenstein for his cookie recipes and opinions. ● Christine Sansom and Preston Batt, who make sure I eat well when I can no longer bear to cook. ● Lucinda Young for her encouragement, support, selfless collaboration and abiding friendship. ● Finally, my parents—who taught me what I wanted to know rather than what they expected me to learn.

Contents

Introduction

Desserts hold a curious place in the synthesis of world cuisines now taking place in America. The European tradition of desserts inherited and so beloved here is nearly absent in the cultures we now routinely raid. In Asia and Africa especially, cooks often mix sweet with sour, salty and bitter throughout a meal and integrate the craving for sugar. We, however, grow up hearing "Not till you've finished your dinner . . ." and learn to earn the sweet by sweating first for our daily bread. Indeed, dessert is often our metaphor for the best of life's pleasures, from the cherry on top to the frosting on the cake. My complaint against traditional American desserts is that, while they often look tasty in their kitsch bliss of squiggly icing and mile-high meringue, they rarely deliver. If all you experience is sugar, you miss the mystery that dessert can hold and sin without true pleasure. ● My own rigorous standard of comparison is informed by a strong Midwestern farm background—a mother who is an accomplished baker and a grandmother whose cooking career began in northern Wisconsin logging camps at 15. I grew up with wild-raspberry-jam-filled cookies and 8 kinds of yeast sweet rolls. After that, all was broken promises—until I went to Europe. The pastries of France with their secrets of flavor and texture made an impression that far outlasted memories of the great art I'd gone to explore. ● After 5 years as an artist and designer in Los Angeles I moved to the still-pristine San Geronimo Valley near San Francisco—to a stream, redwoods and a large garden. There I began to cook, and, as I looked around, it seemed everyone else had too! The Bay Area food revolution was being born. By the time I got to staging elaborate sit-down dinners for guests I hardly knew, I found I had the palate and desire to join the fray myself. As a child I had spent hundreds of happy hours drawing and building architectural fantasies, so the structural nature of pastry in particular appealed to the latent architect in me. I also wanted to achieve the quality of dessert I knew existed but rarely encountered. ● In those early days of nouvelle cuisine, however, desserts were little valued—first ignored as an anachronistic embarrassment, then plundered of their riches in the name of "light dessert." No one endorses wolfing large portions of rich dessert after every meal, but a small, well-flavored indulgence savored is intrinsic to our celebrations. Yet in spite of this there are few notable exceptions to a lack of innovation in the field compared with the exciting achievements in the rest of new American food. Besides a dearth of precedents to draw upon in our favorite exotic cuisines, another reason for this lack may simply lie in the intrinsic differences between dessert and savory cooking. There is far more chemistry involved; to be a good pastry chef is to be a slave to the arcane habits of chocolate, butter, eggs and cream. It's understandable, then, that most pastry chefs are classically trained professionals—and that they become slaves to their techniques and recipes as well, losing their chance for creative freedom. I found the redeeming feature of most dessert components to be that, while volatile in preparation, they are often far more stable at serving time than other foods and more plastic in their range of shapes and forms. Because of this, its heritage of indulgence and ornament and its position in the meal as grand finale, dessert is the opportunity to amaze. ● The architect, graphic artist and cook in me conspired to create a place for myself in the world of pastry. Once asked by a wealthy matron client what cooking school I attended, I hastily replied "L'Ecole aux Frappes Dures," my own high school French for an approximation of "The School of Hard Knocks," to which she responded, "Oh yes, that's in Montreal, isn't it?" "Mmmmm, well, yes, there is a branch there . . ." I sometimes think of myself as one of the great frauds of the San Francisco food world. Not only have I never had the merest shred of formal training, I rarely even use cookbooks. ● At the first pastry job I talked myself into I was left to an occasional scribbled note or recipe taped to the counter, and to my own devices. Between reading, phone calls to Mom, memories of France and help from colleagues I honed a solid repertoire based on my nightly successes in the dining room. (Years later waiters would beg me to return—since they'd presented my glories shortly before the bill, I'd made them good tips.) I interchanged components to expand my range beyond the limits of my education while I broadened my knowledge, eventually compiling a complete kit of versatile basic recipes. ● Since I knew what I'd learned only from experience rather than what I'd been told, I demystified unnecessarily complex cooking procedures and was able to allow my creative side to explore the possibilities of the components I had mastered. The plate became my stage. I began to work with caterers who produce special events, which is more a branch of show business than any other form of food service. ● Most recently I have developed a market for specialty wedding cakes and edible constructions as centerpieces for special events. In one case I made a 4-foot model of San Diego's ersatz Old Globe Theatre from 37 dacquoise cakes, which were assembled on a stage before 300 guests as 37 waiters carried in the pieces on silver trays . . . What should be of interest to the reader in all of this is that my success is based on so little—and that most of it is right here in this book. ● These intensely flavored, richly textured basic recipes are based on historical precedent, but I've made them easy, cogent and reliable. They are the building blocks I use to create an endless variety of stunning new presentations that keep my clients coming back for more. The ideas presented here will have you surpassing the flair of the finest chefs in the profession. Besides the perfect custard or chocolate sauce, your guests will always remember that shard of marbled chocolate or the new experience of eating with a chocolate-dipped spoon. ● Purists in the discipline who might disdain some of the liberties I've taken here would be arrogant in neglecting the most crucial value of all—entertainment. While I have never sacrificed flavor to achieve it and demand only the finest ingredients, I have found that original twists and unfamiliar combinations can add enormously to the social dynamics of any successful gathering. A new experience shared by everyone present is a powerful leveler and, when playful, provides a massive thaw of our normal reserve. Your guests share a conspiracy of privilege at having experienced a delight together—and link that memory inextricably with you, the host who provided it. What I am presenting here, then, is a full spectrum of the elements in my most successful work, and a portfolio of ways they can be combined to create a new style of dessert that deserves all the fantasies, anticipation, childlike wonder and fun that the idea of dessert can conjure. ● Since it is without doubt the most universally irresistible dessert ingredient, chocolate is the theme I have chosen here. This unique, impossible-to-duplicate natural product contains more than 100 chemical compounds, becomes edible only after a long, complex process that includes fermentation, yet contains no alcohol and bears little resemblance to the seed of the rain-forest tree from which it comes. That chocolate is the only food to melt at exactly the temperature of the human mouth is only one of its secrets. Studies have shown compounds found in chocolate to stimulate the brain in a way that duplicates the state of being in love. The desserts in this book can whip up and quell all kinds of passion—and can stimulate the imagination as well. ● A Pacific Heights hostess who recently asked me to prepare a dessert buffet to cap a surprise birthday party for her husband was unsure of success. Not only had she never attempted this kind of event before, there seemed to be lingering doubts as to how well people would mix, coming from all arenas of his life from business to family to social. As it worked out, she related to me by phone the day after the celebration, "I couldn't keep them away from the desserts before he arrived, and then I couldn't get them to eat anything else. They had something to talk about all evening. One big, macho Italian who claimed to never dream of anything but 'naked ladies' just called. He said last night he dreamt instead of your double-dipped strawberries and chocolate mousse!"   ■

Using This Book

There are 23 different dessert presentations pictured in this book. Included in accompanying text is an introduction to the origins of each, a list of equipment needed for assembly, a list of recipe components each contains, an explanation of the assembly procedure plus notes on how to keep them fresh and how many they will serve. Also variously included are further notes of interest and lists of alternate components to try with the desserts. The recipes for the components, numbered 1 through 44, are sorted into six categories—cakes, pastries, fillings and frostings, sauces, little sweets and extras and accents and garnishes.

The desserts contain from 1 to as many as 7 components, but in those with the most components several are additional garnishes in an elaborate display, and are optional. Every effort has been made to scale the yield of each component recipe to the quantity needed for each of the desserts in which it is pictured. However, it's up to you to gauge visually or by measurement its distribution or division into the number of servings you require. This was obviously difficult to standardize for components that are reused many times, but I have been careful to calculate amounts closely to avoid wasteful overage of expensive ingredients. You may choose in some cases to make a full batch when only a portion of one is called for or to double a batch while you're at it for another use. Especially in the case of some sauces or fillings, many of the components are staples that will last for months frozen or simply refrigerated and that can be used as a delicious enhancement to your favorite standards, right down to a simple dish of vanilla ice cream.

In the list of alternate components suggested for many of the desserts the amounts required for that application are not calculated (unless modifications of them are specified). As you gauge such amounts yourself keep in mind that most of these recipes can be at least doubled without diminishing their reliability.

About Notes on Keeping I realize that notes on keeping qualities in recipes here indicate a greater longevity for the finished products than is usually recommended. My estimates are based on solid experience—food for literally hundreds of thousands of people has passed my hands and judgment without a single problem. What I cannot emphasize enough to ensure such a clear record is proper storage and lack of contamination. Generally, hot items, especially those containing eggs and dairy products, should be cooled to room temperature before chilling. Cover foods tightly in clean containers, and never touch them with your fingers, or with contaminated spoons or other implements, after cooking or during storage.

Achieving Dramatic Presentations Although these desserts are pictured in fantasy settings they can transfer to your table with similar effect.

In terms of plates and backgrounds, simple but uncommon ploys can win a lot of attention. When serving a buffet, vary the heights of serving trays with risers; even a napkin-covered cracker box or two will help. Twine the display with loosely draped fabric, ribbons, branches, curios, flowers or candles. For plated desserts, forget all about that tiny disc called the dessert plate. Dessert is an attraction—and demands a venue scaled to its performance. Use standard 10-inch dinner plates for composed presentations, so as not to crowd the action.

The Importance of Precision The use of ruler and X-Acto knife followed me from my experience in graphic design, but it is just as important in culinary design. Take the time to accurately prepare your construction elements and you will end up saving time and trouble, in an effortless assembly. Also, if your base components are precise they more effectively set off free-form elements, such as squiggles of sauce or broken shards of chocolate.

EQUIPMENT NOTES

Hand Tools Most of the hand implements called for here are in any well-equipped kitchen, but in some cases a certain type will be better for pastry than others of its ilk. Large commercial-size rubber spatulas are best for folding, as they disturb the batter least. A heavy, 8-inch metal pastry spatula is essential, and it pays to get a good one. I often call for a slotted wooden spoon since I assume it is more common than a slotted paddle, the tool I prefer for these jobs. As for whisks, any looped wire ones will do, and it may sometimes be convenient to have more than one.

Bowls, Pans and Measuring Cups As a general rule, stainless steel is the preferred substance of both saucepans and bowls in these recipes. It conducts heat well, withstands high temperatures but cools quickly and is nonreactive. Cast iron or aluminum can easily taint delicate custards or acidic fruit sauces. Heavy-walled pots or those with clad bottoms are important to the success of custards made without a double boiler, which is an implement I detest—never the right size, too narrow or too deep, either sputtering steam around the rim or burning dry. I replace it in this book and my life with the appropriate size saucepan of water under the appropriate size stainless steel bowl.

Small, medium and large saucepans referred to here are of 1-, 2- and 3-quart capacities, respectively. Small, medium and large bowl requirements will be easily met by a basic nest of stainless steel bowls, except when a small bowl is used for tinting or dipping small amounts of chocolate. Here a set of custard cups will be useful.

Pyrex is best for measuring cups, especially if you're working with caramelized sugar.

A standard 1-by-12-by-17-inch sheet pan is called for repeatedly here, not from professional bias but because it's the best tool for the job. Heavy-gauge metal construction distributes heat evenly, will not buckle in the oven and provides a perfect surface on the back of the pan for many other uses. The capacity of the commercial-size pan makes it more versatile than the home-kitchen size.

Parchment paper, called for throughout, is the best lining for pans. (A half-sheet of the standard commercial size neatly fits a commercial sheet pan.) Substitutions can be made. Waxed paper can be used for lining cake pans, and freezer paper placed plastic-coated side down can be used on the backs of sheet pans when using them to make garnishes, such as chocolate tiles or filigree. Directions for greasing are particular to each recipe and can't be generalized.

Piping Bags and Tips Three standard plastic or cloth piping bags will be enough to complete any of these creations. Since I abhor most conventional applications of piping anyway, I find the tiny tips sold in cake-decorating kits almost useless. Try larger sizes for more drama; get some unusual tips, and play with their possible effects. There are cake-decorating supply stores in most large cities—I have the incredible good luck to live only a few blocks from one—but suppliers such as the Wilton company offer a complete catalogue for mail order. (Write to Wilton Enterprises Inc., 2240 W. 75th St., Woodbridge, IL 60517.)

The single most useful piping tip I have ever found is the large 2-inch-wide, flat filling tip with one edge toothed and the other smooth. This tip alone has saved me so much time and aggravation that I recommend it exclusively for fillings and for most frosting jobs. The endless spreading and smoothing that overworks filling textures and tears delicate cakes is history, with this simple device.

For instances where a plain, fine stream of sauce or chocolate is called for, the new small, freezer-weight zip-close plastic bags in quart or pint size make ideal piping bags; a corner can be cut to the exact size needed, and the safe closure prevents the contents from spilling backward out of the bag. They can be disposed of or cleaned and reused.

Kitchen Scale Since so many ingredients are measured by weight, in pastry, the scale is an invaluable asset to precise ratios. It is especially useful in measuring nuts and bulk chocolate.

Electric Appliances A KitchenAid, Mixmaster or any electric beater with an attached bowl is an enormous help in any pastry work above the cake-mix level, since long periods of beating are sometimes required. These machines allow you to beat while you proceed with other steps and save your patience for when it's needed.

Food processors have become so ubiquitous in our homes that I employ them regularly in my directions. Key uses for pastry that no other machine can match are creaming butter with sugar or cutting it into flour—tasks even my patient mother was glad to delegate. When a blender can be substituted, this is specified.

INGREDIENTS NOTES

Chocolate With flavors in the foreground, the success of these desserts lies in the impeccable quality of their ingredients. It is unfortunate, then, that the most commonly accessible forms of sweet dark **chocolate** are so dismal, containing large quantities of non-cocoa-based waxes, oils and stabilizers. The basic dark chocolate I use is Guittard dark French vanilla, which I buy in 10-pound blocks. I suggest you use good quality bulk chocolate bought by the pound at your local candy shop and forgo the myriad permutations of supermarket chips and morsels. Even buying it in blocks as I do would not be impractical for the home cook; since cocoa butter stubbornly resists turning rancid, this chocolate will keep for several years. Other types of chocolate used here are unsweetened or baker's chocolate; bittersweet, which contains some sugar; semisweet, which contains a bit more; regular dark sweet chocolate, which is a little sweeter and the most commonly used form; and milk chocolate, which is sweeter yet and contains milk solids as well. Chocolate extract is called for to boost flavor or where graininess would result from use of any other form. Make sure you buy extract, and not an artificial flavoring. As for cocoas, there is usually little commercial choice, but any kind will perform acceptably in these recipes as long as you don't substitute sweetened cocoa.

Finally, there is white chocolate. Yes, I know, it's not really chocolate at all from the viewpoint of the laboratory. But if it looks like chocolate, melts like chocolate and is always used as chocolate is, I think we can take the giddy leap of placing it in the same category—on the continuum beyond milk chocolate, since it is substantially sweeter. Actually, of the two basic white types one is at least a bastard cousin; it contains cocoa butter. This type is slightly translucent and has a yellowish cast and a softer texture. It is therefore not always cooperative in the extreme postures I sometimes ask of it. Then the white pastel coating chocolate stands in. With its palm oil replacing the cocoa butter, it is whiter, more opaque and of a better texture for tinting, spreading and cutting. However for simple dipping procedures you may wish to use the better-flavored cocoa-butter variety. All chocolate should be kept in a dark place, well wrapped, at cool to room temperature.

Other Ingredients All **cream** in these recipes must be heavy whipping cream. Unsalted **butter** is preferred throughout but specified only where nothing else will do. All **milk** referred to in these recipes is whole milk, which, after all, has only 2% more milk fat than does "2%." **Eggs** used here are always extra large, so whatever else you vary in the eggs you choose they must at least be of this same size category to ensure proper ratios, or even appropriate final serving sizes. I use brown, fertile grade AAs produced with no antibiotics or artificial stimulants; of what is available to me they have the best flavor and assure the most consistent performance. The most important point is freshness—for flavor, for loft when whipped, even for separating eggs, since yolks of old eggs tend to collapse. Since eggs are key to the matrix of most of our basic construction materials here, pursuit of the best is no idle quest.

Nuts are often considerably cheaper purchased in bulk at health food stores. If you get more than you plan to use, nuts should be properly stored to avoid having them turn rancid. Pecans, hazelnuts and almonds should be stored in airtight containers and be refrigerated if you plan to keep them more than a few weeks. Nuts with higher oil content and therefore of greater vulnerability, such as pistachios and walnuts, should be kept in the freezer, to be safe. If you buy nuts in small packages, as you need them, make sure they're from a busy store where the stock is likely to turn over regularly.

As for **sugar**, although superfine can sometimes get a better rise out of egg whites, standard granulated sugar has been used in the testing of all these recipes.

Two kinds of **flour** are used in this book: all-purpose unbleached flour and cake flour. In every instance the kind to use is specified. Generally all-purpose is appropriate for its bulk in cookies and pastry; cake flour is useful for its quick disappearing act when being incorporated or in custards that rely on its highly available gluten.

If you have a choice, buy a good quality **vanilla**. It is used here as a basic tool in granting complexity to the flavor of sugar, and I use a lot of it. If all you can get is a common supermarket brand, transfer it to a larger bottle and add a small amount of fine cognac and a vanilla bean to steep.

Very recently a long-standing bastion of tradition has been stormed by those who seek to save us from ourselves; pure **almond extract** is no longer carried in California supermarkets, as a result of the hazardous substances act passed in 1987. Seems the bitter almond oil it is based on contains a trace of arsenic that could conceivably be harmful after your second or third gallon, so we must now content ourselves with artificial almond flavoring.

Finally, a few words about **food coloring**, used here in chocolate decorations and tiles. Artificial coloring is pervasive in the food industry in uses that are totally irrelevant to nature (why must all pickles be dyed that sickly yellow?); at least here the pleasure to the eye and the sense of fun and surprise that color affords is its own reward. Since even a few drops of water can cause chocolate to seize up and become grainy, the highly concentrated commercial paste or powder dyes are essential to creating deep, rich hues. (Paste colors added in large amounts will also cause chocolate to seize, and this can be remedied to a point by whisking in a small amount of oil—never butter, which contains its own moisture. Safflower oil has the least obtrusive taste.) The commercial products are available in cake-decorating supply stores. If you are restricted to liquid supermarket food coloring you will be limited to a pale pastel palette.

TECHNIQUE NOTES

To break bulk chocolate use a heavy, blunt, thick-bladed chef's knife; press the tip straight down into the block, then slowly bring the handle down so the blade acts as a wedge and the chocolate breaks. (In some restaurant is a butcher block imbedded with a half inch of what was once my best paring knife—at once my first act and first mistake as a professional chef.)

To melt chocolate, which scorches easily, use the lowest temperature possible. If you inadvertently scorch chocolate you can still save the good part by shaking it undisturbed through a strainer while still warm. Since the bowl used to melt chocolate is usually used again in the next step, these recipes employ a simple setup of "bowl over saucepan 1/4 full of simmering water" instead of a double boiler for melting (see Equipment Notes), but be sure they fit together well to prevent steam from contaminating the chocolate—water is as great a hazard as high heat.

For dipping remember you must always melt more chocolate than you will use so you will have enough to immerse each object. Just cool and store the overage. This brings us to the **tempering** controversy. The rather alarming whitish surface you sometimes find on chocolate is not from moisture or even old age—it results when the wrong one of two possible configurations of fat crystals forms, usually encouraged by starting at too high a heat and cooling too rapidly. Since it requires the psychic powers of an experienced chocolatier to avoid completely, and is of concern here only in the area of dipped candies when they're kept for a long time, I will not attempt to explore its subtleties. Rest assured that the crystals do not affect flavor or quality, and chocolate so afflicted can be remelted and used again with confidence.

Prepare **nuts** for use according to their type. Pecans and walnuts can be used as they are, but hazelnuts and almonds need to have their skins removed. In the case of hazelnuts this is done by toasting them on a sheet pan in a 350°F oven for about 10 minutes, till they are golden and the skins are loose. Cool them, then rub a few at a time between your palms, holding your hands apart at the bottom so the skins drop out. Almonds have to be blanched. It is easier to buy them blanched than to do it yourself, but if you wish to, pour boiling water over them and soak till cool, then squeeze each nut to slip the seed from its skin. Almonds should then also be toasted before use—again, on a sheet pan in a 350°F oven for 10 minutes (longer if you have just soaked the nuts). I also toast pistachios to crisp them; note this is to no avail unless you then rub them in toweling to remove the excess oil.

Three other basic techniques must be correct to ensure success with these recipes: creaming butter and sugar, whipping egg whites and folding. If you are **creaming butter and sugar** by hand, the butter you start with must be soft enough not to leave lumps but firm enough to avoid melting. The food processor used in recipes here is far more forgiving of cold butter, but one can still risk meltdown by overprocessing, since friction produced by the blade generates its own heat.

The greatest danger in **whipping egg whites** lies in overbeating, causing a dry, crumbling texture that is difficult to fold smoothly. The more sugar used in the given recipe, the longer this state is forestalled—but one must learn visually when to stop beating in a range of instances.

Folding is a technique uniquely important in dessert work yet often the downfall of even many would-be professionals. The process is usually one of combining powdered, ground or liquid ingredients with a matrix into which a great deal of air has been whipped. Since this matrix is likely to be losing its loft anyway from the moment you've stopped beating it, you want to disturb it only as much as is necessary to combine the elements. What you are doing, then, as opposed to stirring, is dragging ingredients through sticky bubbles to cling evenly to them in the wake of your spatula. Plunge the spatula in at a 45° angle just right of center in your bowl, proceed downward to the left at that angle, then follow the contour of the bowl up again at the opposite side of the bowl, flipping the batter you bring up with you over the top. Repeat as you turn the bowl.

As a last word of warning from the voice of experience—always set a timer for everything you put in an oven or leave on a stove-top. ∎

The Components

Cakes

1 *Dark Chocolate Torte*

USE FOR:

Bourbon-Apricot Chocolate Torte

Chocolate Chocolate Mousse Torte

EQUIPMENT:

Large bowl over large saucepan

Electric mixer and bowl

Small bowl

Measuring cup and spoons

Blender or food processor

Whisk

Large rubber spatula

10-inch springform pan, greased and lined with parchment

INGREDIENTS:

8 ounces dark chocolate

1/2 cup unsalted butter

5 eggs

1/3 cup sour cream

1 tablespoon vanilla

1 teaspoon almond extract

1/2 cup toasted blanched almonds (see Technique Notes)

1 tablespoon cake flour

1/2 cup sugar

DIRECTIONS:

1 Melt chocolate and butter together in large bowl over large saucepan 1/4 full of simmering water. Preheat oven to 350°F.

2 While chocolate and butter are melting, separate eggs: whites in the mixer bowl, yolks in the small bowl. Add to the yolks the sour cream, vanilla and almond extract; whisk to smooth.

3 In blender or food processor grind nuts and flour together finely. When the chocolate is completely melted, whisk to smooth and remove from heat. Whisk in egg yolk mixture, then nuts and flour.

4 Beat egg whites in mixer at high speed. As foam turns to fine bubbles, slowly shake the sugar into the bowl in a fine shower. Continue beating till whites are stiff and glossy but not dry.

5 With large rubber spatula fold egg whites 1/3 at a time into chocolate mixture to make a smooth batter.

6 Scrape batter into prepared springform pan; bake at 350°F for 40 minutes.

You may cool and cover torte in pan for further preparation at another time. Or, if proceeding with assembly using torte, let it cool for 10 minutes, then remove sides from pan bottom to cool torte completely.

About Keeping: Torte will keep, frozen, for several months.

Yield: 1 10-inch torte.

14

Chocolate Angel Food Cake

2

INGREDIENTS:

1/2 cup cake flour

1/2 cup cocoa

3/4 cup sugar (with flour mixture)

12 egg whites

1-1/2 teaspoons cream of tartar

1/4 teaspoon salt

3/4 cup sugar (with egg whites)

2 teaspoons vanilla

2 teaspoons chocolate extract

1/2 teaspoon almond extract

DIRECTIONS:

1 Preheat oven to 375°F. Sift together flour, cocoa and 3/4 cup of the sugar. Set aside.

2 In bowl of electric mixer add to egg whites the cream of tartar and salt. Beat till fine bubbles begin to form; then, beating continuously, slowly shake into the egg whites the remaining 3/4 cup of sugar, in a fine steady shower. Beat to stiff-peak stage.

3 Scoop this meringue into large bowl and gently fold in vanilla, chocolate extract and almond extract. Then, disturbing meringue as little as necessary, fold in flour mixture 1/3 at a time, to form a batter.

4 Transfer batter to cake pan by scoops with rubber spatula, taking care not to leave any air pockets while filling. Bake for 30 minutes, till cake is set and springy. Invert to cool, and cool completely before sliding a knife between pan and cake to remove it.

About Keeping: Covered (but not necessarily refrigerated) cake will keep several days.

Yield: 1 10-inch cake.

USE FOR:
Layered Chocolate
Angel Food Cake

EQUIPMENT:
Measuring cups
Sifter
Electric mixer and bowl
Measuring spoons
Large bowl
Large rubber spatula
10-inch tube cake pan, greased
Thin-bladed knife

3 *Chocolate Génoise*

USE FOR:

Chocolate Ribbon Cake

EQUIPMENT:

Medium saucepan

Measuring cups

Sifter

Parchment

Electric mixer and bowl

Whisk

Slotted wooden spoon

Small saucepan

Measuring spoons

Large rubber spatula

Large bowl

Sheet pan 1 by 12 by 17 inches, greased and lined with parchment

Toothpick

Wire rack

NOTES:

Every confection made from a batter is a race against the collapse of air bubbles: a race against time. This is especially true of génoise. While there are few ingredients and they are combined in a few simple steps, easy success demands a deft flow of well-orchestrated moves without interruption. In other words, don't answer the phone. Several thousand batches ago they all laughed at my rubber-bottomed génoise, but the versatile cake soon became one of the fundamentals of my career. These directions describe as accurately as possible what I've learned.

INGREDIENTS:

3/4 cup cake flour

1/4 cup cocoa

1 cup sugar

6 eggs

1/4 cup unsalted butter

2 teaspoons vanilla

1/2 teaspoon almond extract

DIRECTIONS:

1 Preheat oven to 350°F. Heat a few inches of water in medium saucepan over medium heat. (Make sure your mixer's bowl will fit over it stably, well above the water.)

2 Sift flour and cocoa together onto parchment. Measure sugar and have it ready beside the mixer.

3 Break eggs into mixer bowl; whisk to combine. Place bowl over boiling water in saucepan and stir briskly and constantly with slotted wooden spoon till eggs are hot but not curdled. Remove bowl from saucepan and immediately add sugar and begin beating with mixer at high speed.

4 Remove saucepan of water from heat. Reduce heat to low and set over it the butter in small saucepan, to melt. As eggs expand with beating add vanilla and almond extract. When they have reached maximum volume the batter will stop moving up the side of the bowl and, when the beater is lifted, will not run from the tines but fall in a ribbon.

5 Scrape batter into large bowl with spatula. Shake half the flour-cocoa mixture from the parchment over batter and fold in carefully, turning the bowl and scraping the sides. Fold in the other half. Pour butter over batter and fold that in.

6 Scrape batter into prepared pan and bake at 350°F for 15 to 20 minutes, till toothpick comes out clean and cake begins to pull away from edges of pan. Set pan on wire rack to cool. If not using immediately, cake can be wrapped in pan for later assembly.

About Keeping: Will keep several days wrapped and refrigerated; a 1-day rest will actually make cake easier to work with when assembling a dessert. Can also be successfully frozen for several weeks.

Yield: 1 12-by-17-inch cake.

Chocolate Custard Cake

4

INGREDIENTS:

1 cup cocoa

3/4 cup water

2 tablespoons tequila

1/4 cup unsalted butter

1/2 cup sugar

3 eggs

1/2 cup ground, toasted blanched almonds
(see Technique Notes)

1/2 teaspoon Spiced Ground Orange
Peel #41

2 egg whites

DIRECTIONS:

1 Preheat oven to 350°F. In small bowl whisk cocoa, water and tequila till smooth.

2 In food processor cream butter and sugar until light and fluffy. Scrape mixture into bowl of electric mixer and beat in the 3 eggs, then the cocoa mixture. Scrape into large bowl and fold in nuts and peel.

3 Clean and dry mixer bowl and beater for egg whites. Beat them till stiff but not dry; fold into batter. Pour batter into greased loaf pan and bake for 30 minutes. Cake will be baked about an inch or so in but still very soft and gooey in the center; the toothpick test for doneness will not work here. Cool to just slightly warm before running a knife around the edges and turning out to slice. Do not turn out on a cooling rack—since this cake is quite soft it might fall between the wires.

About Keeping: This cake is best soon after baking, but it will still be excellent several days later (although its texture will be more homogenous).

Yield: 1 9-by-5-inch loaf cake; 10 3/4-1-inch slices.

USE FOR:
Mexican Chocolate
Custard Cake

EQUIPMENT:
Small bowl
Measuring cups
Measuring spoons
Whisk
Food processor
Rubber spatula
Electric mixer and
bowl
Large bowl
1-quart-capacity
loaf pan, greased

17

Pastries

5 *Almond-Hazelnut Meringue*

EQUIPMENT:

Wide pastry brush

1-by-12-by-17-inch sheet pan

Parchment

Food processor

Measuring cups

Electric mixer and bowl

Large bowl

Large rubber spatula

NOTES:

This crisp, nutty sheet of meringue is my favorite building material, since it can easily be cut into shapes and provides a rigid base for exotic decoration. I have used it for everything from a leaping rainbow trout for the 85th birthday of an avid fly fisherman to a 6-foot edible reproduction of the Golden Gate Bridge, complete with chocolate cars, for a bank reception. In this book it makes two appearances—as the heart of the Lightning Bolt Dacquoise (page 64) and the base of the Meringue and Chocolate Checkerboard buffet (page 80) display.

INGREDIENTS:

2 tablespoons melted butter

8 ounces almonds, blanched and toasted (see Technique Notes)

4 ounces hazelnuts, toasted and rubbed to remove skins (see Technique Notes)

1/4 cup unbleached all-purpose flour

1-1/2 cups sugar (with nuts)

8 egg whites (freeze yolks or just refrigerate them to reserve for another use)

1/4 cup sugar (with egg whites)

DIRECTIONS:

1 Preheat oven to 400°F. Brush sheet pan with melted butter, line with parchment and brush again.

2 In a food processor combine both kinds of nuts, flour and 1-1/2 cups sugar; process till mixture looks like coarse meal.

3 Beat egg whites with mixer at high speed, and once at soft-peak stage slowly and gently shake in 1/4 cup sugar. Beat to stiff-peak stage.

4 Scrape egg whites into large bowl with spatula, and fold in nut mixture 1/3 at a time to form batter. Scrape into prepared pan and spread with spatula 1/2 inch deep as evenly as possible.

5 Bake in 400°F oven for 25 minutes, till top is browned and meringue pulls away from sides of pan and feels firm to the touch. Cool for 10 minutes, turn out on another sheet of parchment and peel paper off back of the meringue. Allow to cool completely before continuing.

About Keeping: Once cool, meringue may be cut, wrapped and stored a few days or even frozen before you assemble your presentation.

Yield: 1 12-by-17-inch meringue.

Chocolate Pastry Dough

6

INGREDIENTS:

2 cups unbleached all-purpose flour

3 tablespoons cocoa

3 tablespoons sugar

1/2 cup unsalted butter, cold

1/4 cup lard or solid shortening

1/3 cup cold water

DIRECTIONS:

1 Sift flour, cocoa and sugar together into food processor. Cut butter into chunks, add to flour mixture with lard and process just to cut in thoroughly.

2 Add cold water and process till dough begins to form a ball. Press dough into 2 equal flat discs. Wrap and refrigerate at least 1/2 hour before working, to allow the gluten to relax.

About Keeping: You can store dough up to 2 weeks frozen.

Yield: Pastry for 2 9-inch pie shells, 1 9-inch 2-crust pie, or 16 3-inch tart shells.

USE FOR:
Chocolate-Hazelnut Pie
Chocolate-Pastry-Latticed Apricot Pie
The Tomlin Tart

EQUIPMENT:
Measuring cup and spoons
Sifter
Food processor
Plastic wrap

Chocolate Sandwich Cookies

7

INGREDIENTS:

1 cup sugar

3/4 cup unsalted butter

2 eggs

1 teaspoon vanilla

2 cups unbleached all-purpose flour

1/3 cup cocoa

3/4 teaspoon baking soda

1/4 teaspoon salt

DIRECTIONS:

1 Preheat oven to 350°F. In food processor cream sugar and butter. Add eggs and vanilla; process to smooth.

2 Scrape mixture into medium bowl. Sift together flour, cocoa, baking soda and salt. With heavy wooden spatula work dry ingredients into butter-egg mixture till it forms a solid mass. Shape dough into a flat square.

3 Roll out lightly floured dough on lightly floured board to be roughly 14 by 14 inches and 1/4 inch thick. With ruler and paring knife cut pastry into 16 3-by-3-inch squares (4 up and 4 across). With metal spatula slide them onto ungreased baking sheets.

4 Bake at 350°F for 10 minutes. Remove to wire cooling rack with metal spatula. The cookies must of course be completely cooled before using.

About Keeping: Wrap or bag cookies if you are not using them right away, so they'll remain moist and cakey when paired with the ice cream.

Yield: 16 3-by-3-inch cookies (for 8 ice cream sandwiches).

USE FOR:
Chocolate Chip–Mint Ice Cream Sandwiches

EQUIPMENT:
Food processor
Measuring cups and spoons
Medium bowl
Sifter
Heavy wooden spatula
Rolling pin
Pastry board
Ruler
Paring knife
Metal spatula
Sheet pans
Wire rack

8 *Striped Refrigerator Cookies*

INGREDIENTS:

1 cup unsalted butter

3/4 cup sugar

1 egg yolk

1 teaspoon vanilla

1/4 teaspoon almond extract

2-1/2 cups unbleached all-purpose flour

2 ounces unsweetened chocolate, melted and cooled

DIRECTIONS:

1 In food processor cream butter and sugar. Add egg yolk and vanilla; process to smooth.

2 Measure half—about 3/4 cup—of this mixture into medium bowl. Add almond extract, then 1-1/4 cups of the flour. Stir them in with heavy wooden spatula, then work dough with hands into a flat, square mass. Wrap in plastic and set aside.

3 Put second half of butter mixture in bowl and whisk in chocolate. Add the second 1-1/4 cups of flour. Stir in with wooden spatula, then work dough with hands to form a flat rectangle. Wrap and refrigerate.

4 On lightly floured board roll out vanilla half of dough into a 9-by-9-inch square, 1/4 inch thick. With ruler and knife trim top edge, then slice into 4 2-inch strips 9 inches long. Remove to back of sheet pan with long metal pastry spatula. (If strips stick to board, put a little flour at the front end of the spatula.)

5 On lightly floured board roll out chocolate half of dough into a rectangle about 9 by 11 inches, 1/4 inch thick. With ruler and knife trim narrow edge, then slice the rest into 5 strips 2 inches wide and 9 inches long.

6 Starting with the chocolate strip closest to you brush surface with water. Using long metal pastry spatula lift 1 of vanilla strips and place on top of chocolate strip. Repeat, alternating colors and brushing with water between each layer; finish with last chocolate strip. Press down to seal the layers.

7 Wrap completed log of layered dough tightly in plastic wrap and refrigerate several hours. To bake, preheat oven to 350°F, cut dough in 1/4-inch slices, lay on ungreased sheet pan and bake 10 to 15 minutes. If some layers separate, place them together on pan and they will join while baking. Lift with metal spatula and cool on rack.

About Keeping: Baked cookies will keep well, but if you don't need them all at once bake only as many as you want; keep remainder of dough, refrigerated, as long as 2 to 3 weeks.

Yield: About 32 cookies.

Chocolate Shortbread

9

NOTES:

British friends insist shortbread can't be made properly without rice flour, but since the finely milled variety they use is not available here you had best stick to all-purpose flour. Rice flour, because it is gluten free, is thought to form a more crumbly texture. In any case the gluten in our regular wheat flour will find little cause for excitement in this method of preparation.

INGREDIENTS:

2 cups unbleached all-purpose flour

1/4 cup cocoa

2/3 cup powdered sugar

1 cup unsalted butter

DIRECTIONS:

1 Preheat oven to 350°F. Sift together into food processor the flour, cocoa and sugar.

2 Cut butter in 1-tablespoon pieces and add to flour mixture. Process till butter is just cut in and mixture looks like coarse meal. Do not overprocess.

3 Dump mixture into baking pan, smooth to an even layer and press in with fingers. Bake at 350°F for 20 minutes. If making plain shortbread remember to cut into squares before it cools. If making Chocolate-Hazelnut Shortbread Squares, continue with directions under Assorted Cookies and Sweets, page 104.

About Keeping: Shortbread will keep several weeks; in fact, flavor improves as butter ages a bit.

Yield: 32 squares.

USE FOR:
Chocolate-Hazelnut Shortbread Squares (Assorted Cookies and Sweets)

EQUIPMENT:
Sifter
Measuring cup
Food processor
9-by-13-by-2-inch baking pan, greased

Chocolate Tortellini

10

INGREDIENTS:

1 cup all-purpose flour

3 tablespoons cocoa

3 tablespoons powdered sugar

1 egg

2 tablespoons water

1 tablespoon chocolate extract

1/3 cup sweetened chestnut purée

1/3 cup ricotta cheese

1/4 cup ground toasted almonds (see Technique Notes)

1 egg yolk

DIRECTIONS

1 Measure flour, cocoa and sugar into food processor; pulse till combined.

2 Add egg, water and chocolate extract; process till mixture forms a ball. With floured hands remove dough. Form into a flat square, wrap it in plastic and refrigerate at least 1/2 hour, to relax dough before rolling.

3 In small bowl blend chestnut purée, ricotta cheese, ground almonds and egg yolk. Set aside.

4 On lightly floured board roll out dough into an approximately 20-by-20-inch square. With pastry cutter cut 36 rounds of pasta. Pull background scraps away and discard.

5 Place 1 teaspoon of the filling on each round. Spray surfaces with a mist of water, fold each in half and pinch edge to seal. Pull the two points toward each other across the back fold, and pinch together. Repeat with all 36, transferring each to wire-mesh rack as completed. Freeze.

6 When ready to serve, drop tortellini into a large pot of rapidly boiling water and cook for 3 to 5 minutes or till al dente.

About Keeping: Tortellini should be frozen, then bagged until ready to use (or the moisture in the cheese will migrate into the pasta and ruin it). Will keep 2 to 3 weeks frozen and, once cooked, minutes.

Yield: 36 tortellini; 6 servings of 6 each.

USE FOR:
Chocolate Tortellini in Pear Broth

EQUIPMENT:
Measuring cups and spoons
Food processor
Small bowl
Pastry board
Rolling pin
2-1/2-inch-diameter round pastry cutter
Spray bottle
Wire-mesh rack
Pasta pot

11 *Chocolate Chip Eclairs*

USE FOR:

Custard-filled Chocolate Chip Eclairs

EQUIPMENT:

Small bowl

Whisk

Measuring cup

Heavy-bottomed medium saucepan

Slotted wooden spoon

Electric mixer and bowl

Rubber spatula

Piping bag with large star tip

Cold, buttered sheet pan

NOTES:

Make a double batch of these and freeze some—they reheat well and are excellent with many other fillings. Keep the chips of chocolate small, or they will make holes in the surface of the pastry when they melt (and allow gases to escape and defeat the puffing).

INGREDIENTS:

2 eggs

1/4 cup unsalted butter

1/2 cup water

1/2 cup unbleached all-purpose flour

1 tablespoon finely chopped dark chocolate

DIRECTIONS:

1 Break eggs into small bowl and whisk slightly to combine.

2 In medium saucepan heat butter and water to boiling over medium-high heat; add flour and beat with wooden spoon till mixture forms a ball and comes away from the sides of the pan.

3 Dump dough into mixer bowl and begin beating at medium speed, adding eggs in a stream. Continue beating after eggs are incorporated till texture changes from sloppy to smooth, thick and sticky. Scrape batter into the egg bowl, cover and refrigerate 1 hour or till cold enough not to melt chocolate. If you plan to proceed preheat oven to 400°F, but batter will keep a day at this point.

4 Fold chopped chocolate into cold batter. Fill piping bag fitted with large star tip with batter, and pipe out the 6 5-inch-long éclairs onto cold, buttered sheet pan, turning the bag as you pipe to create a spiral effect. (If the pan isn't cold the butter will be slippery, the dough will slide away from you as you pipe and you will lose control of the shape.)

5 Bake at 400°F for 30 minutes or until golden brown. Slice open lengthwise to allow excess moisture to escape.

About Keeping: What you have to defeat here is the migration of moisture from the interior to what you wish to remain a crisp exterior. Therefore, if serving in a few hours leave uncovered; if keeping a day or longer freeze and recrisp in a 400°F oven for about 10 minutes, to be sure the moisture stays where you want it.

Yield: 6 éclairs.

Chocolate Crêpes

12

NOTES:

It is so easy to turn out crêpes once you're set up for it, and they freeze so well, I recommend you make more than you need and store the rest for another time and another filling. Be forewarned: the first one never works. If it sticks, clean the pan thoroughly and be sure it's back up to temperature before trying again.

INGREDIENTS:

1 cup unbleached all-purpose flour

1/4 cup cocoa

1/4 cup sugar

3 eggs

1 teaspoon vanilla

1 teaspoon chocolate extract

1-1/2 cups milk

Butter, for frying

DIRECTIONS:

1 In blender or food processor combine flour, cocoa, sugar, eggs, vanilla and chocolate extract; add milk in a stream while machine is running. Refrigerate 2 hours or overnight before making crêpes.

2 To fry, heat crêpe pan to medium high and wipe with a wad of paper towel smeared in butter. Using a small ladle pour about 1-1/2 ounces of batter into the pan, immediately tilting the pan to cover the bottom with the thinnest possible sheet of batter. Adjust the amount you pour according to the amount required to just cover.

3 Cook 1-1/2 to 2 minutes on first side, till browned. Turn crêpe over, cook 1 minute more and turn out. Repeat, occasionally wiping the pan with more of the butter; use only enough to keep crêpes from sticking. Stack completed crêpes with strips of parchment or waxed paper between them. Wrap and refrigerate until you fill them.

About Keeping: Refrigerated, batter keeps 2 days; cooked crêpes, 1 week. Frozen crêpes keep several months.

Yield: 18 to 20 crêpes.

USE FOR:
Chocolate Crêpes with Flambéed Oranges

EQUIPMENT:
Measuring cup and spoons
Blender or food processor
6-inch crêpe pan
Small ladle
Parchment or waxed-paper strips to separate crêpes

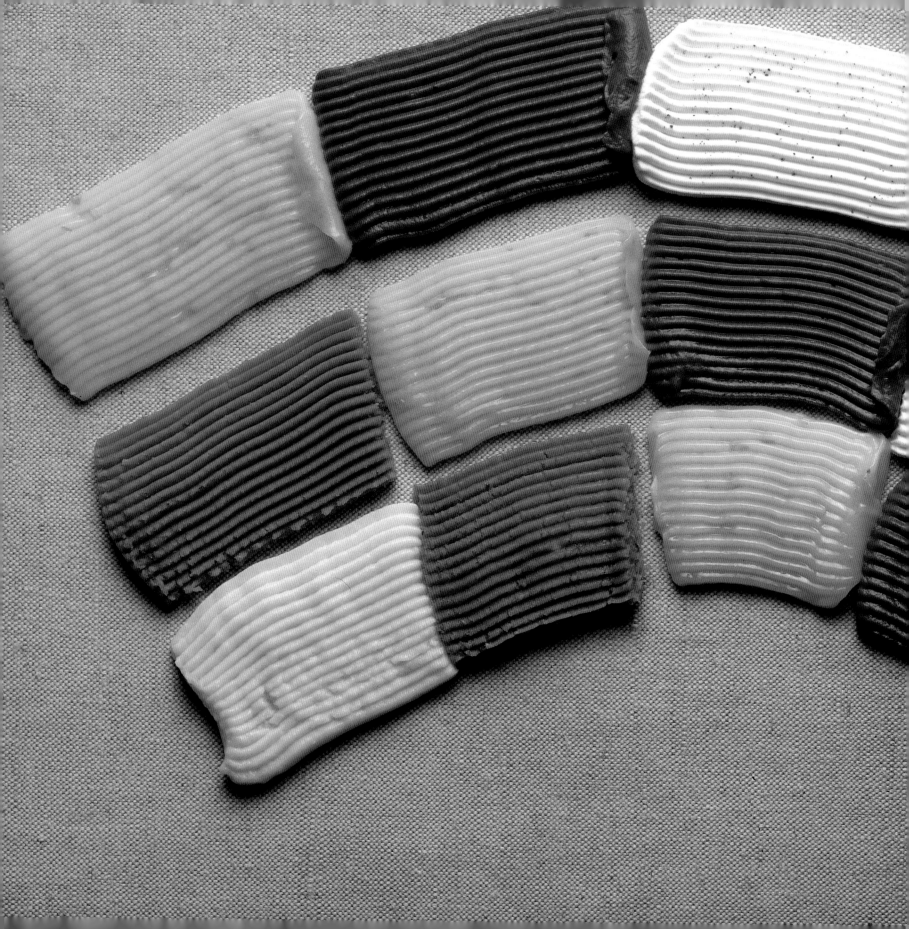

Fillings & Frostings

13 *Dark Chocolate Mousse*

USE FOR:

Chocolate
Chocolate Mousse
Torte

Meringue and
Chocolate
Checkerboard

EQUIPMENT:

Medium bowl over
medium saucepan

Knife

Electric mixer and
bowl

Small bowl

Whisk

Measuring spoons

Large bowl

Large rubber
spatula

Measuring cup

NOTES:

Keys to success here are the gradual cooling of the chocolate as various ingredients are added, the texture of the egg whites and your folding technique; if the whites are too stiff you will tend to overfold to incorporate them. If necessary live with a few flecks of white rather than risk loss of loft.

INGREDIENTS:

1 pound dark chocolate

1 cup unsalted butter

8 eggs

2 tablespoons sugar

1/2 cup heavy cream

DIRECTIONS:

1 In medium bowl over medium saucepan 1/4 full of simmering water, melt chocolate.

2 While chocolate is melting, cut butter in small chunks and separate eggs: whites in mixer bowl, yolks in small bowl.

3 Whisk chocolate to smooth. Remove bowl and saucepan from heat, add butter and whisk till all lumps are melted.

4. Remove bowl from saucepan and whisk in egg yolks till smooth.

5 Use mixer to beat egg whites, adding sugar slowly as they reach soft-peak stage. Stop when they are stiff but not dry.

6 Scrape chocolate mixture into large bowl, and fold in egg whites 1/3 at a time.

7 In mixer bowl whip heavy cream till stiff. Fold into mousse. Refrigerate; about 2 hours to use as torte filling or at least 4 hours to set (best set overnight).

About Keeping: Will keep, refrigerated, up to a week.

Yield: 5 cups mousse.

Spiced Mascarpone

INGREDIENTS:

12 ounces Mascarpone cheese

1 tablespoon finely chopped crystallized ginger

1 tablespoon honey

2 teaspoons Frangelico liqueur

1/2 teaspoon Spiced Ground Orange Peel #41

1/2 teaspoon cinnamon

1/4 teaspoon nutmeg

1/4 teaspoon ground cloves

DIRECTIONS:

1 Measure all ingredients into bowl and fold in with rubber spatula.

2 Refrigerate to refirm cheese; it will thin considerably as you work it. But don't worry—it will scoop.

About Keeping: Will keep up to a week.

Yield: 1-1/2 cups spiced Mascarpone.

USE FOR:

Chocolate Crêpes with Flambéed Oranges

Chocolate Ribbon Cake

Layered Chocolate Angel Food Cake

Meringue and Chocolate Checkerboard

Poached Pears with Gold Leaves

EQUIPMENT:

Measuring spoons

Medium bowl

Rubber spatula

Bourbon-Apricot Filling

INGREDIENTS:

2/3 cup bourbon whiskey

8 ounces dried apricots

1/4 cup sugar

1/4 cup water

DIRECTIONS:

1 Combine whiskey and dried apricots in food processor. Pulse till roughly chopped, but hang on—it will be a bumpy ride.

2 Scrape fruit into saucepan, add sugar and water and bring to a boil over medium-high heat. Reduce to low and simmer 5 minutes, stirring occasionally but avoiding the fumes. (They can be intoxicating in the literal sense.)

3 Cover the pot, remove from heat and do not disturb until cooled completely. Scrape into storage container and chill before using.

About Keeping: Will keep for several months, refrigerated.

Yield: About 1-1/2 cups filling.

USE FOR:

Bourbon-Apricot Chocolate Torte

Chocolate Chip–Mint Ice Cream Sandwiches

Chocolate Chocolate Mousse Torte

Layered Chocolate Angel Food Cake

EQUIPMENT:

Measuring cup

Food processor

Rubber spatula

Medium saucepan with lid

Spoon

16 *Coffee Buttercream*

USE FOR:

Chocolate Chip–
Mint Ice Cream
Sandwiches

Lightning Bolt
Dacquoise

EQUIPMENT:

Electric mixer
with bowl
and paddle
attachment

Measuring cups
and spoons

Rubber spatula

Sifter

NOTES:

This is the only kind of buttercream I can bear, the bitter coffee cutting the high sugar-fat content. I recall once early in my career making a bride-to-be cry when I said raspberry buttercream frosting would make her guests gag and they'd all want coffee instead of champagne. I've learned a little about client relations since then, though I've still managed to avoid making an oversweet buttercream wedding cake. And whenever I do use buttercream, I put the coffee in it myself.

INGREDIENTS:

1-1/2 cups unsalted butter, softened

2 tablespoons heavy cream

2 tablespoons good-quality instant coffee granules

1 teaspoon water

2 egg yolks

2 cups powdered sugar

DIRECTIONS:

1 Beat softened butter in mixer with paddle attachment till smooth. Beat cream in.

2 Dissolve instant coffee in water. Add coffee and egg yolks to butter and beat till well mixed, scraping sides of bowl.

3 Sift powdered sugar and add half at a time to the butter mixture, combining at low speed first to avoid a sugar-coated kitchen. Finish at high speed, beating till smooth. Wrap and refrigerate if you don't plan to use it right away, but remember you will have to return it to room temperature before you can work with it again.

About Keeping: Can be kept a week refrigerated or be frozen.

Yield: 2 cups buttercream.

Apricot Pie Filling

17

INGREDIENTS:

4 1-pound cans pitted apricots in heavy syrup

2 tablespoons brandy

2 tablespoons cornstarch

1/2 cup sugar

1/4 teaspoon almond extract

DIRECTIONS:

1 Open cans and drain fruit in large strainer over medium bowl.

2 Measure 2/3 cup of the drained syrup into medium saucepan. Discard rest of syrup and transfer apricots to bowl.

3 In measuring cup combine brandy and cornstarch; whisk to smooth, and scrape into saucepan. Stir in sugar and almond extract, heat to boiling over medium heat and boil 1 minute. Stir thickened syrup into fruit; cool before filling pie so you won't melt the pastry!

About Keeping: Can be made up to a week before making pie and refrigerated.

Yield: About 4 cups pie filling; will fill a 9-inch pie.

USE FOR:
Chocolate-Pastry-Latticed Apricot Pie

EQUIPMENT:
Can opener
Large strainer
Medium bowl
Measuring cups
Medium saucepan
Measuring spoons
Small whisk
Rubber spatula

Flambéed Oranges

18

INGREDIENTS:

6 to 8 oranges, preferably large, meaty, deeply colored navels or Valencias—to equal 3 cups pulp after preparation

1-1/3 cups Grand Marnier

1/3 cup sugar

DIRECTIONS:

1 Cut off both ends of each orange to the flesh and pare off all the skin. Cut orange in half lengthwise, then cut a deep V inside each half to remove core and thick area of membrane where sections meet. Push out any seeds. Place each half flat side down; cut into thirds lengthwise and then across in 1/2-inch slices.

2 Heat Grand Marnier in sauté pan over medium-high heat, ignite with a match and add orange slices at once. Shake pan to mix and burn off all the alcohol. When flame dies and oranges are heated through transfer them with slotted metal spatula to storage container.

3 Add sugar to Grand Marnier, stir and reduce to a thick syrup. Pour sauce over oranges. Serve in crêpes.

About Keeping: Can be refrigerated up to 2 days (serve at room temperature).

Yield: About 3 cups; fills 12 crêpes.

USE FOR:
Chocolate Crêpes with Flambéed Oranges

EQUIPMENT:
Sharp paring knife
Measuring cup
Large sauté pan
Slotted metal spatula

19 *Vanilla Custard Filling*

USE FOR:

Chocolate Ribbon Cake

Custard-filled Chocolate Chip Eclairs

Layered Custard Cream Parfaits

Meringue and Chocolate Checkerboard

Poached Pears with Gold Leaves

The Tomlin Tart

EQUIPMENT:

Measuring cup

Sifter

2 medium bowls

Whisk

Measuring spoons

Heavy-bottomed 3-quart saucepan

Rubber spatula

Slotted wooden spoon

Plastic wrap

NOTES:

This custard is a well-flavored, thick-textured building material with many uses. It will support layered cakes without slipping and fill pastry with less sogging than do alternatives. If you're left with a few lumps when through cooking pick them out or live with them—do not attempt to strain this after cooking or you will break the matrix of the molecules and it won't be as firm. Also be sure to use cake flour, which is more finely milled; the greater surface area of its particles makes the gluten more available, and it is more tenacious.

The one time I thought these things wouldn't matter I ended up at a party wiping gobs of filling from the sides of a cake that had disgorged half its contents on a tide of slippery custard. Even the dozen skewers with which I had impaled the cake had failed to staunch the flow of disaster, with 30 minutes left before the arrival of the guests. I simply cleaned the ooze, straightened the tilt, repiped the sides and covered the top with flowers. (This is the only delivery problem I have ever had, and you are sworn to secrecy.) They thanked me later for a delicious cake, but I didn't take another private commission for 6 months.

INGREDIENTS:

1/3 cup plus 1 tablespoon cake flour

3/4 cup sugar

2 cups milk

6 egg yolks

2 teaspoons vanilla

1/4 teaspoon almond extract

DIRECTIONS:

1 Sift flour into sugar in one medium bowl, and whisk together to mix completely.

2 In another medium bowl whisk 1/2 cup of the milk into the egg yolks. Then whisk that mixture into the flour-sugar suspension, until it is completely smooth and the sugar is dissolved. Whisk in vanilla and almond extract.

3 Heat the rest of the milk in heavy-bottomed saucepan over medium-high heat. Just as the milk boils, whisk half of it into the egg-flour mixture, then scrape all of that back into the pot.

4 Immediately begin stirring with slotted wooden spoon, and stir constantly till custard begins to thicken. The price of not using a double boiler is eternal vigilance.

5 As custard thickens it will go through a lumpy stage. Don't be alarmed, but pick up the speed of your stirring and beat the custard with the slotted spoon—and wear a mitt, since the mixture can spatter and will be hot. Continue to beat and it will smooth out and thicken just before boiling. Stir and boil for 1 minute.

6 Immediately remove from heat and scrape into storage container, covering the surface with plastic wrap to prevent a skin from forming. Allow to cool before refrigerating. Can be used as soon as it's cold.

About Keeping: Will keep up to a week, refrigerated.

Yield: 3 cups custard.

Chocolate Custard Filling

20

INGREDIENTS:

1/3 cup cake flour

1/4 cup cocoa

3/4 cup sugar

2 cups milk

6 egg yolks

2 teaspoons vanilla

1/4 teaspoon almond extract

1/2 teaspoon chocolate extract

DIRECTIONS:

1 Sift flour and cocoa into sugar in 1 medium bowl, and whisk together to mix completely.

2 In the other medium bowl whisk 1/2 cup of the milk into the egg yolks. Then whisk that mixture into the flour-sugar suspension, until it is completely smooth and the sugar is dissolved. Whisk in vanilla, almond and chocolate extract.

3 Heat the rest of the milk in heavy-bottomed saucepan over medium-high heat. Just as the milk boils, whisk half of it into the egg-flour mixture, then scrape all of that back into the pot.

4 Immediately begin stirring with slotted wooden spoon and stir constantly till custard begins to thicken. Not using a double boiler does exact the price of eternal vigilance.

5 As custard thickens it will go through a lumpy stage. Don't be alarmed, but pick up the speed of your stirring and beat the custard with the slotted spoon— and wear a mitt, since the mixture can spatter and will be hot. Continue to beat, and it will smooth out and thicken just before boiling. Stir and boil for 1 minute.

6 Immediately remove from heat and scrape into storage container, directly covering the surface with plastic wrap to prevent a skin from forming. Allow to cool before refrigerating. Can be used as soon as it's cold.

About Keeping: Will keep up to a week, refrigerated.

Yield: 3 cups custard.

USE FOR:

Chocolate Ribbon Cake

Custard-filled Chocolate Chip Eclairs

Layered Custard Cream Parfaits

Meringue and Chocolate Checkerboard

Poached Pears with Gold Leaves

EQUIPMENT:

Measuring cup

Sifter

2 medium bowls

Whisk

Measuring spoons

Heavy-bottomed 3-quart saucepan

Rubber spatula

Slotted wooden spoon

Plastic wrap

21 *Chocolate-Hazelnut Pie Filling*

USE FOR:

Chocolate-Hazelnut Pie

Chocolate-Hazelnut Shortbread Squares (Assorted Cookies and Sweets)

EQUIPMENT:

Large chef's knife

Food processor

Measuring cup

Rubber spatula

Medium bowl

Whisk

INGREDIENTS:

8 ounces hazelnuts, toasted and rubbed to remove skins (see Technique Notes)

3/4 cup dark brown sugar

1/2 cup unsalted butter

3 eggs

2 ounces unsweetened chocolate, melted and cooled

1/2 cup light corn syrup

2 teaspoons vanilla

2 tablespoons Frangelico liqueur

DIRECTIONS:

1 Lightly chop hazelnuts. You can pulse them in a food processor, but I prefer to chop by hand with a large, heavy knife to better control the size of the pieces. Larger bits are nicer in the pie; if making hazelnut squares, smaller pieces will make them easier to cut.

2 In food processor cream brown sugar and butter. Add eggs and chocolate; process to smooth.

3 Scrape mixture into medium bowl. Whisk in corn syrup, vanilla and liqueur. Stir in nuts. From here follow assembly for Chocolate-Hazelnut Pie, page 96, or Chocolate-Hazelnut Shortbread Squares, page 105.

About Keeping: Use immediately.

Yield: About 4 cups filling.

22 *Tangerine Curd*

USE FOR:

Custard-filled Chocolate Chip Eclairs

Layered Chocolate Angel Food Cake

Meringue and Chocolate Checkerboard

Mexican Chocolate Custard Cake

EQUIPMENT:

Medium bowl over medium saucepan

Measuring cup

Small bowl

Whisk

Rubber spatula

Plastic wrap

NOTES:

Try this twist on traditional lemon curd with other frozen fruit juice concentrates.

INGREDIENTS:

1/2 cup unsalted butter

1/2 cup sugar

4 ounces tangerine juice concentrate

Zest of 2 tangerines (optional)

2 whole eggs

4 egg yolks

DIRECTIONS:

1 In bowl over saucepan 1/4 full of simmering water, melt butter with sugar, juice concentrate and zest. Whisk to smooth.

2 In small bowl, whisk eggs and egg yolks together; stir into hot mixture. Continue to stir with rubber spatula, scraping sides and bottom of bowl. Curd will go through a lumpy stage but smooth out again as it thickens. When thickening stops in 5 to 10 minutes remove curd to storage container, apply plastic wrap directly to surface to prevent skin forming and cool before refrigerating.

About Keeping: Will keep up to a week, refrigerated.

Yield: About 2 cups curd.

White Chocolate Ganache

NOTES:

Crème fraîche helps cut the sweetness of the white chocolate, although you may use heavy cream to replace it.

INGREDIENTS:

8 ounces white chocolate

2/3 cup crème fraîche

DIRECTIONS:

1 In small bowl over medium saucepan 1/4 full of simmering water melt chocolate. Whisk to smooth.

2 Remove bowl from saucepan and whisk in crème fraîche. Allow it to cool till its texture is suitable to use; for piping, you may want to refrigerate it briefly.

About Keeping: Can be stored refrigerated for up to 6 weeks; remelt and cool to bring to proper working texture.

Yield: 1-2/3 cups ganache.

USE FOR:

Bourbon-Apricot Chocolate Torte

Chocolate Ribbon Cake

Layered Chocolate Angel Food Cake

Lightning Bolt Dacquoise

EQUIPMENT:

Small bowl over medium saucepan

Measuring cup

Whisk

Dark Chocolate Ganache

NOTES:

An alternate to this recipe's food processor method for melting the chocolate with the cream is use of a bowl over hot water. However, to melt that last lump of chocolate over water takes so much more heat that the ganache takes much longer to cool enough to use.

INGREDIENTS:

8 ounces dark chocolate

1/2 cup heavy cream

2 tablespoons light corn syrup

DIRECTIONS:

1 Chop chocolate into small chunks and load into food processor.

2 Heat cream to boiling and pour immediately over chocolate in food processor. You may want to hold a towel around the lid of the machine to start—it is initially a rough and splattery ride. Process until all the lumps of chocolate have been melted. Add corn syrup and pulse to combine. The ganache will be a perfect consistency for glazing cakes; a few minutes' refrigeration will bring it to piping texture.

About Keeping: Can be stored refrigerated for up to 6 weeks; remelt and cool to bring to proper working texture.

Yield: 1-1/2 cups ganache.

USE FOR:

Bourbon-Apricot Chocolate Torte

Layered Chocolate Angel Food Cake

Lightning Bolt Dacquoise

Meringue and Chocolate Checkerboard

EQUIPMENT:

Heavy knife

Food processor

Small saucepan

25 *Whipped Cream*

EQUIPMENT:

Electric mixer and
bowl, chilled

NOTES:

It may seem presumptuous to offer a recipe for one of the first things a child is allowed to do in the kitchen. Yet few things are so often done badly—oversweetened, overwhipped or abandoned completely for aerosol or even ersatz versions. These proportions and hints will make every batch pipe like silk, dollop like a cloud and last for hours if it has to. In what must have been its ultimate test, a whipped-cream-covered five-tier wedding cake for more than 500 people remained intact in a garden gazebo in August at 97°F for 3-1/2 hours one recent summer. I can think of no higher recommendation; it's served me well.

INGREDIENTS:

1 cup heavy cream, well chilled

1 tablespoon powdered sugar

1 teaspoon vanilla

DIRECTIONS:

1 The most crucial thing to remember is to whip slowly. The electric mixers that bade farewell to the ache in whisking arms gave us more power than we need when it comes to cream, and we use too much. Beat at medium speed—the air bubbles trapped between the fat molecules will be finer, stronger and more durable and will achieve greater loft.

2 As soon as the first faint ridges left in the wake of the tines appear on the surface of the cream, add first the powdered sugar, then the vanilla. The cornstarch in the powdered sugar will be all you'll need of a stabilizer. Whip to texture appropriate for use intended.

About Keeping: Don't let my anecdote about the wedding cake act as license to abuse—whipped cream should be kept cold as long as possible before serving. While it will hold piped for several hours it should be whipped just before piping to ensure a smooth flow. If it must stand for even a few minutes before entering the piping bag, whisk first to smooth.

Yield: About 2-1/3 cups whipped cream.

Whipped Crème Fraîche

26

NOTES:

Prepared crème fraîche is now available in some markets; if not in yours, it's easy enough to make at home. Buttermilk provides the culture to thicken the cream. Because crème fraîche is thicker to begin with it whips to only about half the volume of the same amount of cream uncultured.

INGREDIENTS:

1/4 cup buttermilk

1 cup heavy cream

2 tablespoons powdered sugar

DIRECTIONS:

1 Mix buttermilk with heavy cream in jar and cover loosely just to keep out dust. Set in a warm but not hot place for 24 hours, till mixture is thick but drops from a spoon in fine strings.

2 Cover and chill; it will thicken more when cold.

3 To whip, add powdered sugar and beat at medium speed. It will look thinner at first, then develop a stiff-peak texture heavier than that of whipped cream.

About Keeping: Crème fraîche whipped and refrigerated will keep up to a week; whipped, for several hours. Although it should always be whipped as close to serving time as possible, it does maintain a better texture longer than whipped cream.

Yield: 1-2/3 cups whipped crème fraîche.

USE FOR:

Chocolate Crêpes with Flambéed Oranges

Chocolate Ribbon Cake

Fruit and Cream with Chocolate Triangles

Layered Chocolate Angel Food Cake

Mexican Chocolate Custard Cake

Poached Pears with Gold Leaves

EQUIPMENT:

Measuring cup

1-pint glass jar

Measuring spoons

Electric mixer and bowl

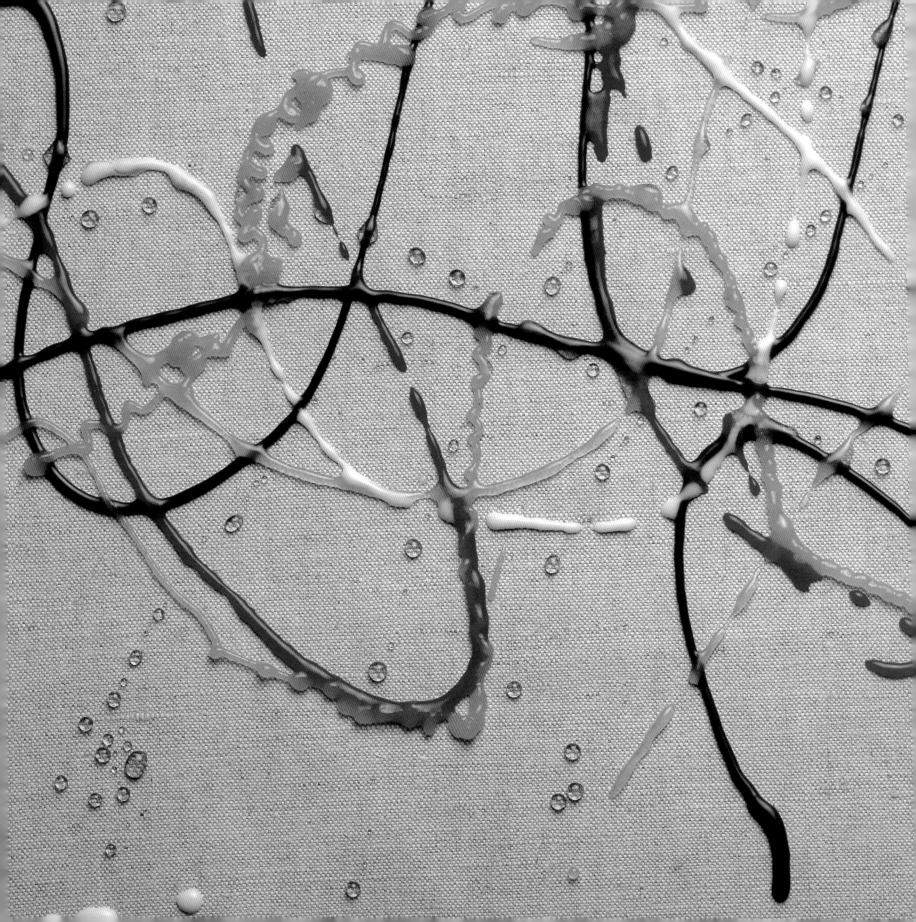

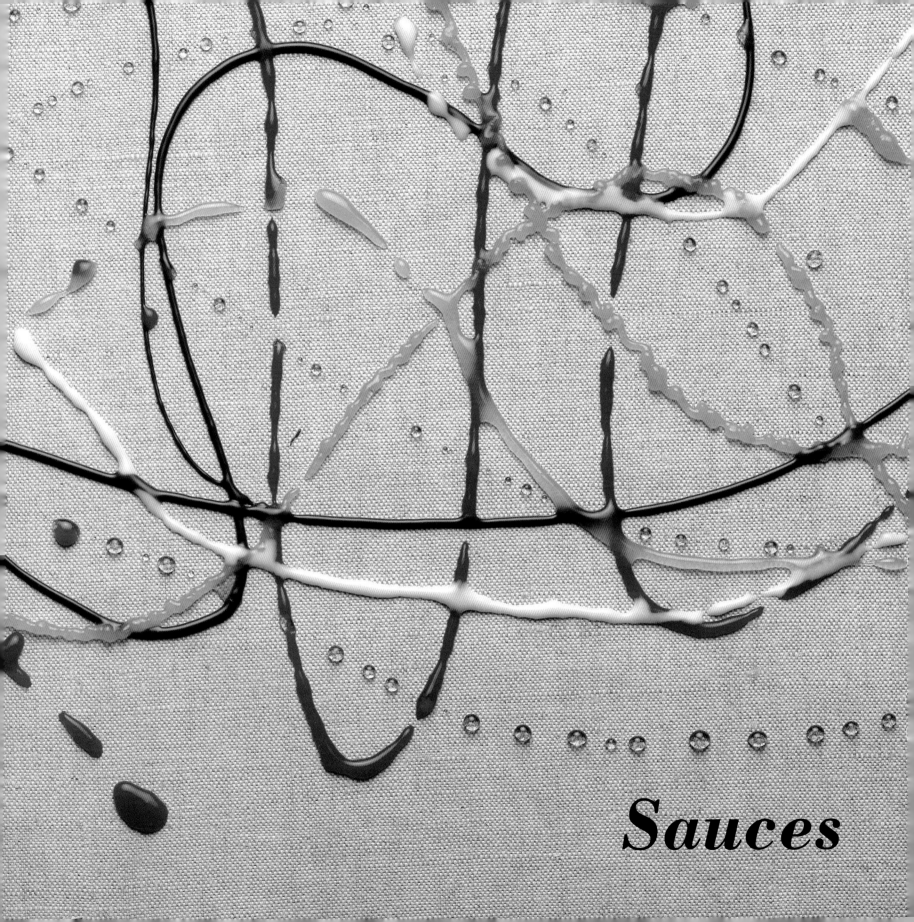

Sauces

27 *Chocolate-Cognac Sauce*

USE FOR:

Custard-filled Chocolate Chip Eclairs

Joan Collins' Broken Heart

Poached Pears with Gold Leaves

EQUIPMENT:

Medium bowl over medium saucepan

Whisk

Measuring cup

Measuring spoons

INGREDIENTS:

8 ounces dark chocolate

1/2 cup milk

2 tablespoons light corn syrup

2 tablespoons cognac

DIRECTIONS:

1 In medium bowl over medium saucepan 1/4 full of simmering water melt chocolate.

2 Whisk in milk till smooth, then corn syrup and cognac.

3 Warm to slightly above room temperature to serve; sauce should pour but not spread on plate.

About Keeping: Will keep for up to 6 weeks, refrigerated.

Yield: About 1-3/4 cups sauce.

28 *Bitter Orange Sauce*

USE FOR:

Joan Collins' Broken Heart

Mexican Chocolate Custard Cake

Mocha Mousse with Bitter Orange Sauce

Poached Pears with Gold Leaves

Raspberries with Custard and Fruit Sauces

EQUIPMENT:

Small saucepan

Measuring cup

Measuring spoons

Wooden spoon

NOTES:

"Bitter" here refers not to the fruit called the bitter orange but to this sauce's sharp flavor. Its lack of sweetness allows it not only to cut the sweetness of other components in a dessert but to make a terrific addition to meat glazes and marinades.

INGREDIENTS:

1 6-ounce can frozen orange juice concentrate, thawed

1/3 cup sugar

1 tablespoon Grand Marnier

DIRECTIONS:

1 In small saucepan combine thawed concentrate, sugar and Grand Marnier.

2 Stir ingredients and bring to a boil over medium-high heat; stir at full boil for 2 minutes or till sauce is reduced to 3/4 cup.

3 Chill before using.

About Keeping: Will keep for several months, refrigerated.

Yield: 3/4 cup sauce.

Raspberry Sauce

29

NOTES:

This is the most luxurious of all fruit sauces, for here we cheat nature by removing the thorns on the rose of the fruit world—the seeds of the raspberry. Most raspberry sauces depend so much on sugar and thickening agents to achieve proper texture that they dull the fruit's naturally sharp flavor. Here the sauce is thickened with the pulp of the berries themselves, creating a fruity, velvety, gleaming sauce worth making for the scent in your kitchen alone! Remember all fresh raspberries are not created equal; you may need to reduce the sauce more or less depending on their moisture content.

INGREDIENTS:

2 1/2-pint baskets fresh raspberries

2 tablespoons water

1/4 cup sugar

2 tablespoons light corn syrup

DIRECTIONS:

1 Put raspberries and water in saucepan and bring to a boil over medium heat. Use wooden spoon to stir in sugar, and cook for 5 minutes, till berries are completely broken down.

2 Pour berries into strainer over small bowl; allow to cool. Then press through as much of the remaining juice and pulp as possible, till nothing remains in strainer but dry seeds. You may use a spoon or rubber spatula for this, but your best tool here is your fingers, rubbing the pulp up the sides of the strainer. Occasionally scrape the accumulation on the underside into the juice. You may need to repeat this to remove all the seeds; if you do, whisk strained raspberries first.

3 Whisk the pulp and juice together with the corn syrup, and return to saucepan. Cook over medium heat another 10 minutes to clear sauce and reduce it to 1 cup. Put in storage container and refrigerate. Serve cold.

About Keeping: Will last up to 2 weeks, refrigerated, but if reboiled weekly will last several weeks longer.

Yield: 1 cup sauce.

USE FOR:

Chocolate
Chocolate Mousse Torte

Custard-filled Chocolate Chip Eclairs

Joan Collins' Broken Heart

Layered Custard Cream Parfaits

Mango and Chocolate Sorbets

Mexican Chocolate Custard Cake

Mocha Mousse with Bitter Orange Sauce

Poached Pears with Gold Leaves

Raspberries with Custard and Fruit Sauces

EQUIPMENT:

Small saucepan

Measuring spoons

Measuring cup

Wooden spoon

Strainer just fine enough to hold seeds back

Small bowl

Whisk

30 *Apricot Sauce*

USE FOR:

**Joan Collins'
Broken Heart**

**Mexican Chocolate
Custard Cake**

**Raspberries
with Custard
and Fruit Sauces**

EQUIPMENT:

Can opener

Measuring cup

**Food processor or
blender**

Rubber spatula

Medium saucepan

Wooden spoon

Strainer

Measuring spoons

NOTES:

This piquant, velvety fruit sauce is so versatile it even finds its way into my Oriental stir-fry sauces, where it not only lends its flavor but acts as a thickening agent as well.

INGREDIENTS:

1 16-ounce can pitted apricot halves in heavy syrup

1 tablespoon brandy

DIRECTIONS:

1 Open canned apricots and drain syrup into measuring cup.

2 In food processor or blender, combine apricots with 1/2 cup of the syrup. Purée till completely smooth.

3 Scrape into medium saucepan and bring to boil over medium heat. Cook for 5 minutes, stirring occasionally with wooden spoon, to reduce to 1-1/2 cups of sauce.

4 Strain into storage container, then stir in brandy. Refrigerate and serve cold.

About Keeping: Will keep for several months, refrigerated.

Yield: 1 cup sauce.

Vanilla Custard Sauce

NOTES:

This is one of the more difficult basic sauces to master only because it's one of those where you know you had it right only after you've already cooked it too long. It should be as thick as it can get without curdling the egg and making it grainy—it should never boil. If you have gone so far that even the whisking over ice water doesn't help to return its luster, a trip through a food processor may still work.

INGREDIENTS:

1-1/3 cups milk

2 teaspoons vanilla

5 egg yolks

1/2 cup sugar

DIRECTIONS:

1 Scald milk in heavy-bottomed medium saucepan, just till skin forms. Remove from heat and add vanilla.

2 With electric mixer beat egg yolks and sugar at high speed till they are nearly white. Add 1/3 of the hot milk and beat slowly to combine.

3 Return milk and egg yolks to the milk in the saucepan. Cook over medium-low heat, stirring constantly with slotted wooden spoon, till sauce thickens slightly and holds a line drawn with your fingertip in a coating of sauce on the back of a metal spoon.

4 When sauce is done transfer to the bowl partially immersed in ice water and stir further, to reduce the temperature rapidly and stop the cooking. Pour into a storage container and refrigerate.

About Keeping: Will keep up to a week, refrigerated.

Yield: About 2 cups sauce.

USE FOR:
Mexican Chocolate Custard Cake
Poached Pears with Gold Leaves
Raspberries with Custard and Fruit Sauces

EQUIPMENT:
Measuring cup
Heavy-bottomed medium saucepan
Measuring spoons
Electric mixer and bowl
Slotted wooden spoon
Metal spoon
Medium metal bowl partially immersed in ice water

Little Sweets & Extras

32 *Bourbon Prunes in Chocolate*

USE FOR:
Assorted Cookies and Sweets

EQUIPMENT:
Measuring cup

Steep-sided small bowl

Medium sauté pan

Slotted metal spatula

Wire rack over sheet pan

Small bowl over saucepan

Whisk

Parchment

Small 4-ounce cup or ramekin

Wooden skewer

INGREDIENTS:

1/2 cup bourbon whiskey

6 ounces (about 20) large pitted prunes

1/4 cup sugar

4 ounces milk chocolate

DIRECTIONS:

1 Pour whiskey into steep-sided bowl, add prunes and soak for 24 hours.

2 Dump whiskey and prunes into sauté pan, add sugar and bring to boil over medium heat. Ignite and burn off alcohol, shaking pan constantly.

3 Turn heat to low; continue to reduce liquid, shaking pan occasionally, 10 minutes.

4 As glaze gets thick and sticky and begins to caramelize remove prunes with slotted metal spatula. Drain on wire rack over sheet pan, and cool.

5 In small bowl over saucepan 1/4 full of simmering water melt chocolate. Whisk to smooth.

6 Remove wire rack, scrape drips of sugar off sheet pan and line with parchment. Scrape chocolate into small cup to make dipping easier. Spear each prune with the skewer, dip 2/3 into chocolate, lift, shake and place on parchment. Allow to set in cool place. Do not refrigerate (moisture condensation loosens and spots chocolate).

About Keeping: This candy will be at its most attractive served soon after dipping. Can be kept in an airtight container for several weeks; though chocolate may discolor, flavor will not be affected.

Yield: About 20 dipped prunes.

Pistachio Brittle on Chocolate

INGREDIENTS:

4 ounces shelled pistachios

1/4 cup water

3/4 cup sugar

1 tablespoon butter for brittle

1/4 teaspoon baking soda

About 1/2 tablespoon butter for sheet pan

6 ounces bittersweet chocolate

DIRECTIONS:

1 Spread nuts on sheet pan and place in 350°F oven for 5 to 10 minutes to toast lightly. Dump onto towel and rub to blot excess oil. Wipe off sheet pan and rub with butter.

2 Measure water, then sugar into saucepan on stove—do not move or stir these, to prevent any sugar crystals from sticking to sides. Bring to boil over medium heat, and continue to cook without stirring till sugar caramelizes—watch carefully.

3 As sugar reaches a golden brown color remove from heat and at once stir in with wooden spoon nuts, remaining tablespoon butter and baking soda—mixture will foam up. Begin spooning small clusters of nut brittle on buttered sheet pan; form about 20. Cool at least 15 minutes, till candy is hard and cool enough to be handled.

4 In small bowl over small saucepan 1/4 full of simmering water melt chocolate. Stir to smooth. Line second sheet pan with parchment and spoon onto it 1-inch dollops of chocolate—as many as you have nut clusters. Loosen clusters by twisting. Wipe bottom of each on towel to remove butter and push it into a pool of melted chocolate till chocolate shows around the edge. Allow to set in a cool place before peeling off parchment.

About Keeping: Can be kept in an airtight container several weeks, stored in a cool, dark place.

Yield: About 20 candies.

USE FOR:
Assorted Cookies
and Sweets

EQUIPMENT:
2 sheet pans
Towel
Measuring cups
and spoons
Medium saucepan
Wooden spoon
Parchment
Small bowl over
small saucepan
Spoon

34 *Poached Pears*

USE FOR:

Chocolate
Tortellini in Pear
Broth

Poached Pears
with Gold Leaves

EQUIPMENT:

Paring knife

Medium bowl

Vegetable peeler

Melon baller

Large saucepan
with lid

Slotted spoon
(if necessary)

Sheet pan
(if necessary)

NOTES:

No other fruit reaches our markets in such a bewildering array of varieties, from the delicate juicy Bartletts through the buttery Comices to the sturdy Boscs and d'Anjous. Any of these can be used here, though the softer types or very ripe pears of any variety require greater care in handling to prevent scarring (bruises do not go away) and a far shorter cooking time. As a general rule pears of less than out-of-hand eating ripeness are best and the firmer varieties like Bosc and d'Anjou the most reliable. But all pears beg to be poached, for two important reasons. Since they brown and bruise easily, they need the double protection of being kept from the air and being slightly candied by the sugar. And although the flesh retains its shape well when cooked, the sponge-like texture has a tendency to dissipate pears' moisture content; so it is best to cook and store them suspended in liquid until serving to keep them plump, firm and juicy.

Although pears are most often poached in red wine, I find the color unpleasant after they are drained for serving and dry off a bit, and the color doesn't completely penetrate, which causes problems if you need to trim, slice or fan the fruit for presentation. A perfect match is found in wedding the flavors of pear and Chardonnay, and the mellow golden color the pears assume is very appealing.

For enough poaching liquid to make Chocolate Tortellini in Pear Broth (page 66), double the amounts of wine and cinnamon and add pear nectar (you'll still have 4 extra pear halves; use them to top green salads with toasted nuts and a tart dressing).

INGREDIENTS:

2 lemons

5 medium well-shaped pears

1 bottle (about 3-1/4 cups) white wine, preferably Chardonnay

1 stick cinnamon

3/4 cup sugar

For Chocolate Tortellini in Pear Broth:

3 cups (2 12-ounce cans) pear nectar

DIRECTIONS:

1 Halve and squeeze the lemons into the medium bowl, which you've half-filled with water, and throw in the rind.

2 To prepare pears, cut off stems and pare out blossom ends. Peel pears; a paring knife is fine, but a vegetable peeler gets smoother results. Halve them, scoop out seed pocket with melon baller, and remove stem fibers with a V-shaped notch cut from hole to stem end. Put each half immediately in lemon water as completed.

3 In large saucepan heat to boiling the wine, cinnamon and sugar (and pear nectar, if making Chocolate Tortellini in Pear Broth). Add pears and, if necessary, some of the lemon water to cover. Bring back to a simmer, cover and cook till pears can be pierced with a fork at the seed cavity but are still firm—from 5 to 20 minutes, depending on ripeness and variety.

If pears are just right at this point, remove saucepan from heat and allow to cool uncovered before transferring to a storage container for refrigerating. Or if they have already started to get soft and can be easily pierced with a fork, lift out each pear half carefully with a slotted spoon and lay it out on a sheet pan to cool quickly; cool the poaching liquid separately, before adding it to pears for storage.

About Keeping: Will keep several weeks, refrigerated.

Yield: 10 poached pear halves.

Molded Mocha and Cream Mousse

35

INGREDIENTS:

1/4 cup water

1 tablespoon unflavored gelatin

1-1/4 cups milk

1/3 cup sugar

4 egg yolks

1 teaspoon vanilla

2 tablespoons good-quality instant coffee granules

2 teaspoons chocolate extract

1 cup heavy cream

DIRECTIONS:

1 Measure water into a small bowl and stir in gelatin. Set aside to soften.

2 In medium saucepan heat milk. Meanwhile in second small bowl whisk sugar vigorously into egg yolks. As milk forms a skin whisk 1/3 of it into the egg yolk mixture, then scrape that back into the saucepan of milk and whisk to combine.

3 Cook and stir with wooden spoon over medium heat till mixture thickens slightly and holds a line drawn with your fingertip in a coating of it on the back of the spoon. Remove from heat, add softened gelatin and stir till gelatin is completely dissolved.

4 You now have 2 cups of custard base. Measure 1/2 cup of this into the first small bowl, and add 1/2 teaspoon of the vanilla. Pour the rest into second small bowl and stir in coffee, chocolate extract and the other 1/2 teaspoon of vanilla.

5 With electric mixer whip cream till stiff. As plain vanilla custard begins to cool and thicken, fold in 1/2 cup of the whipped cream. Pour this into the bottom of slightly wet mold. Refrigerate.

6 As mocha custard begins to cool and thicken fold in the rest of the whipped cream. As soon as the vanilla mousse has set enough to support it fill the rest of the mold with mocha mixture. Cover and refrigerate overnight before unmolding.

About Keeping: Will keep for several days in mold, refrigerated.

Yield: 4 cups mousse (6 servings of 2/3 cup).

USE FOR:
Mocha Mousse with Bitter Orange Sauce

EQUIPMENT:
Measuring cups and spoons

2 small bowls

Medium saucepan

Whisk

Rubber spatula

Wooden spoon

Electric mixer and bowl

1-quart-capacity mold

36 *Coeur à la Crème Mixture*

USE FOR:
Joan Collins'
Broken Heart

EQUIPMENT:
Food processor
Measuring cups and spoons
Electric mixer and bowl
Large bowl
Large rubber spatula

INGREDIENTS:

8 ounces cream cheese

8 ounces cottage cheese

1/3 cup powdered sugar

1 tablespoon vanilla

3 tablespoons Amaretto liqueur

1 cup heavy cream

DIRECTIONS:

1 Pinch cream cheese in small lumps into food processor with cottage cheese, powdered sugar, vanilla and Amaretto. Pulse 6 to 8 times, then run machine till mixture is fairly smooth but still grainy.

2 In electric mixer whip cream to stiff-peak stage.

3 Scrape cheese mixture into large bowl and fold in whipped cream.

To mold the mixture, proceed with instructions under Joan Collins' Broken Heart (page 102).

About Keeping: To preserve texture that results when mixture sets, it should be molded at once.

Yield: Sufficient for 1-quart mold.

37 *Chocolate Chip–Mint Ice Cream*

USE FOR:
Chocolate Chip–
Mint Ice Cream
Sandwiches

EQUIPMENT:
Electric mixer and bowl
Medium saucepan
Measuring cup
Rubber spatula
Wooden spoon
Measuring spoons
1-quart ice cream freezer
2 1-quart square plastic freezer containers, 3-1/2 by 3-1/2 inches

INGREDIENTS:

2 eggs

2/3 cup sugar

1-3/4 cups milk

2 cups heavy cream

1 tablespoon vanilla

1/2 teaspoon mint extract

6 drops liquid green food coloring

1/2 cup finely chopped dark chocolate

DIRECTIONS:

1 With electric mixer beat eggs and sugar till nearly white.

2 In medium saucepan heat milk just till skin forms. Beat 1/3 of it into egg-sugar mixture, then stir that back into the milk remaining in the saucepan.

3 Cook over medium heat and stir constantly with wooden spoon till custard thickens slightly and holds a line drawn with your fingertip in a coating of sauce on the back of the spoon. Chill thoroughly for several hours.

4 Stir in cream, vanilla, mint extract, food coloring and finely chopped chocolate. Pour into ice cream maker and follow machine directions. (It will fit fine,

even though the finished product exceeds 1 quart.) Pack finished ice cream into the square plastic freezer containers.

About Keeping: Will keep indefinitely in the freezer.

Yield: 1-1/4 quarts ice cream (8 slices, 3 by 3 by 3/4 inches, for ice cream sandwiches).

Chocolate Sorbet

INGREDIENTS:

1/2 cup sugar

1 cup water

2 tablespoons chocolate extract

1/2 cup evaporated milk

2 egg whites

1/2 cup heavy cream

DIRECTIONS:

1 In medium saucepan over medium heat bring sugar, water and chocolate extract to boil; cover, reduce heat and simmer 5 minutes. Uncover and cook 1 minute more, then add evaporated milk. Transfer to medium bowl and chill for several hours before proceeding.

2 With electric mixer beat egg whites till soft peaks form. Fold cream into egg whites, then egg whites into chocolate mixture in medium bowl.

3 Pour into ice cream freezer and follow machine directions.

About Keeping: Will keep indefinitely in the freezer.

Yield: 3 cups sorbet.

USE FOR:
Mango and Chocolate Sorbets
Poached Pears with Gold Leaves

EQUIPMENT:
Medium saucepan with lid
Measuring cups and spoons
Medium bowl
Rubber spatula
Electric mixer and bowl
1-quart ice cream freezer

Mango Sorbet

INGREDIENTS:

1/2 cup sugar

1 cup water

1 ripe mango

3 tablespoons lemon juice

1/2 cup heavy cream

DIRECTIONS:

1 In medium saucepan over medium heat combine sugar and water and bring to boil; cover, reduce heat and simmer 5 minutes.

2 Cut mango in half around the stone, and scrape pulp from seed and skin to measure 1 cup. If you have less add water. Purée pulp with simmered sugar water in blender, then scrape through strainer with rubber spatula to remove tough fibers. Stir in lemon juice, then cream. Chill thoroughly for several hours.

3 Pour into ice cream freezer and follow machine directions.

About Keeping: Will keep indefinitely in the freezer.

Yield: 3 cups sorbet.

USE FOR:
Chocolate Chip–Mint Ice Cream
Sandwiches
Mango and Chocolate Sorbets

EQUIPMENT:
Medium saucepan with lid
Measuring cups and spoons
Paring knife
Blender
Strainer
Rubber spatula
1-quart ice cream freezer

Accents & Garnishes

40 *Chocolate Tiles*

NOTES:

Since I developed this versatile component several years ago it has become my trademark; I never seem to run out of new designs and applications, and there are so many left I doubt if I ever will. It has been everything from a sort of chip with dessert dips to "frosting" to garnish, and never fails to elicit an amazed, delighted response.

"Tiles" are any shape you cut or break from a base sheet of chocolate, which you create as described here. The sheet may be of dark, white or tinted chocolate and be top-decorated or not. Sheet-top decorations may be the drizzle, stripes, marble effect, gilding or smears you're guided here to reproduce or be any other design that you invent.

Because dark chocolate has a lower melting temperature than white it is more difficult to work with in this form, and its uses are restricted. Among these recipes it's called for only in Joan Collins' Broken Heart; the fact that this dessert is kept cold makes the use of dark chocolate more practical. The material that offers most flexibility, especially when you use an X-Acto knife to cut precise shapes, is pastel coating chocolate. It contains no cocoa butter at all but is similar in look and taste to chocolate that does and is far superior in handling—smooth and firm, not brittle.

What follows are directions for creating the basic chocolate sheet, then additional directions for achieving each of the variations pictured in this book, followed by directions for cooling and then cutting and breaking the sheet into tiles. Though the technique is straightforward, working with chocolate always requires attention to detail; please read through the directions once before you start.

INGREDIENTS:

Small amount vegetable oil

8 to 9 ounces white or dark chocolate, for 1 base sheet plain chocolate

Food coloring (preferably commercial paste or powder; see Ingredients Notes)

For Adding Sheet-top Decorative Chocolate:

2 ounces extra chocolate for each color (the minimum for convenient melting; actually apply no more than 4 ounces total)

DIRECTIONS:

To Make a Base Sheet:

1 Smear back of sheet pan with the oil, then top with pan-sized sheet of parchment so it clings to the pan but has no oil on top. Be sure parchment has no ridges or air bubbles.

2 In bowl over saucepan 1/4 filled with simmering water melt chocolate. You'll need 1 bowl each for white and dark chocolate if using both, but you can melt their contents one at a time as called for in variations. Whisk to smooth.

For tinted white chocolate add color. First ladle any white chocolate that

you're tinting for sheet-top decoration only into one or more small cups. Then, if using paste, with toothpicks or skewers transfer a very small amount (it's strong!) into each cup of chocolate, and stir with spoon to blend color completely.

3 Scrape smoothed warm chocolate onto parchment. It is a good idea—especially in first attempts—to warm the pan over a stove-top burner slightly to extend working time. With metal pastry spatula spread chocolate to all corners and then from end to end from both long sides, to create a smooth layer of chocolate slightly less than 1/8 inch thick.

4 With white or tinted white chocolate only, once you've spread a smooth layer proceed with a variation, A through E, if desired. Note that all the variations require a still-soft base sheet except those that use gold, for which the base sheet should be cooled thoroughly before the application.

To Vary the Base Sheet:

A To Apply Dark Chocolate Drizzle (as for Fruit and Cream with Chocolate Triangles, page 90): Put small amount melted dark chocolate in heavy-plastic bag, and cut small hole in corner. While chocolate base sheet is still soft, pipe on a random pattern of drizzle. Do not tap pan to smooth as in variations using white sheet-top chocolate; since dark chocolate is softer, tapping would cause the sheet to break along the lines of the drizzle.

B To Apply Marbleizing (as in Layered Chocolate Angel Food Cake, page 94): Use small amounts extra melted chocolate that you've tinted one or more contrasting colors; dip fingertip in each color and fling it at the still-soft base sheet to form spatter patterns. Then draw a skewer through the entire surface in random patterns to swirl and "pull" the colors. If the chocolate has already begun to set, warm the pan over burner to resoften. Rap the pan smartly on the edge of your work table, and any irregularities in the surface will smooth out.

C To Apply Stripes for Drawn Stripes or Zigzags: Scrape each sheet-top chocolate tint you're using into a small, heavy-plastic bag; cut a small hole in corner of each and pipe alternating stripes across the length of the pan into the still-soft base sheet.

For drawn stripes (as in front half of Lightning Bolt Dacquoise, page 64) draw a skewer through the stripes in a series of loops a few stripes wide from end to end. Repeat all the way down and across the pan.

For zigzag effect (as in Raspberries with Custard and Fruit Sauces, page 78) draw skewer in a repeating-W pattern across a few stripes at a time along the length of the pan; then come back across the pan a short distance beneath the first line in the opposite direction; then reverse and go back again to the bottom of the sheet. If you get this far, believe me, it's better than finger painting.

Rap sheet pan sharply on the edge of your work table to smooth any surface irregularities.

D To Apply Contrasting Smears (as on one garnish for Layered Custard Cream Parfaits, page 100): Use extra melted white chocolate that you've tinted one or more contrasting colors; drip these in small amounts at random points across the base sheet. With metal pastry spatula smear chocolate back and forth from end to end, from each long side of the pan. You'll have only 2 or 3 passes before the colors begin to muddy, so make them count.

E To Gild or Accent with Gold: Gold for gilding may be found at graphics or art supply stores catering to designers and sign makers. It is edible; that is, it's inert—it doesn't combine with anything in the body and passes through. Though difficult to deal with and hard to find, gold instills like nothing else a sense of wonder and luxury. It has been used as a garnish in India for centuries. The easiest form to use comes attached to squares of parchment, said to be for "gilding in the wind" —ask for it.

To gild (as for Poached Pears with Gold Leaves, page 98) lay the gold-covered parchment gold side down on a well-set chocolate base sheet. Rub your finger carefully back and forth across the back of the sheet; the gold will adhere to the surface of the chocolate.

To accent tiles with gold (as in one of the garnishes on Layered Custard Cream Parfaits, page 100) first cut individual tiles so you know where you want the gold to go. Lay the gold-covered parchment over tiles gold side down, and with a pencil point, draw a zigzag pattern onto each tile to press a line of the gold onto the surface of the chocolate. Lift the paper and brush off excess gold.

To Cool the Completed Sheet and Cut or Break into Tiles:

Put chocolate sheet in a cool place to set. With dark chocolate, once it's maximally set at room temperature you may need to refrigerate it momentarily to make it firm enough to cut. Never refrigerate either form of white chocolate, however. Either form will pick up moisture or, as it returns to room temperature, water will condense on it; this may spot the chocolate and will make colors run.

To cut into tiles use a ruler and X-Acto knife, found in art supply or hobby shops. If you're not used to using one, be careful—they are very sharp! If the finished chocolate tile has curled in cooling carefully rewarm it over a stove-top burner on its pan just enough to relax it before laying on the ruler. When you remove cut pieces remember to peel off any parchment that may be stuck to the back.

To break into tiles lift entire sheet of chocolate, peel back parchment and break off pieces.

About Keeping: Will keep several weeks covered in a cool, dark place. (Dark chocolate may develop visible bloom.)

Yield: 1 base sheet. See dessert recipes for number of sheets necessary for the sizes and shapes of tiles required.

EQUIPMENT:

12-by-17-inch sheet pan with flat bottom

Parchment

Medium bowl (or bowls) over medium saucepan

Whisk

Rubber spatula

Metal pastry spatula

For Adding Tints:

Toothpicks or small skewers

Spoon for each color

For Handling Sheet-top Decorative White Chocolate:

Ladle

Small cups for mixing colors

Also:

Small, heavy-plastic bags for piping (variations A and C)

Gold (variation E; see note there)

41 Spiced Ground Orange Peel

USE FOR:

Chocolate Crêpes with Flambéed Oranges

Chocolate Tortellini in Pear Broth

Poached Pears with Gold Leaves

EQUIPMENT:

Vegetable peeler

Parchment-lined sheet pan

Electric coffee/ spice grinder

NOTES:

This gorgeous, saffron-colored powder is useful in desserts, as a garnish or even in most savory cooking where a hint of orange is desired. If you find particularly well colored oranges make more—it will keep until you use it up.

INGREDIENTS:

3 to 4 large, well-colored oranges

1/2 teaspoon ground cardamom

DIRECTIONS:

1 With vegetable peeler (which allows the precise control of thickness you need) cut orange part of skin from the oranges. Lay strips on parchment-lined sheet pan with outer skin side up and put in 250°F oven for 30 minutes or until they are crisp when cool, but not browned. Open oven a few times to release moisture and let the fragrance into the kitchen!

2 When cool combine with cardamom in spice grinder and grind to a fine powder.

About Keeping: Lasts indefinitely if kept in freezer.

Yield: 2 tablespoons ground peel.

42 Chocolate Filigree

USE FOR:

Layered Custard Cream Parfaits

Poached Pears with Gold Leaves

EQUIPMENT:

Small bowl over saucepan

12-by-17-inch sheet pan

Parchment

Rubber spatula

Small, heavy-plastic bag

NOTES:

This is perhaps the easiest garnish here for the amount of drama it produces. There is no need to spend hours perfecting exact replicas of classic fans and rosettes. Naively drawn atoms, stars, lattice or just an overall Jackson Pollock squiggle and spatter that's randomly broken can be far more interesting.

INGREDIENTS:

3 ounces chocolate

Few drops vegetable oil

DIRECTIONS:

1 In bowl over saucepan 1/4 full of simmering water melt chocolate. Smear back of sheet pan with vegetable oil and smooth a pan-sized sheet of parchment onto it.

2 Scrape chocolate into plastic bag. Cut a very small hole at corner; test thickness of line it produces and increase size of hole as needed to achieve the effect you desire. Pipe out filigree designs—enjoy yourself!

3 Set chocolate in a cool place to firm, but do not refrigerate. Lift parchment and peel back to free shapes or break pieces off filigree sheet.

About Keeping: Make the same day as serving; in time, chocolate may discolor.

Yield: 1 sheet filigree.

Chocolate Decorations

43

NOTES:

Unlike flat chocolate tiles this form of chocolate decoration allows 3-dimensional effects. It is also easier in this form than others to use dark chocolate, if you'd like, though possibilities for tinting are more limited. The decorations will attach readily to most dessert surfaces; whipped cream would be too wet, but ganache, buttercream or chocolate makes a fine base.

INGREDIENTS:

4 ounces chocolate, white or dark

For tinted white chocolate, paste food colorings (see Ingredients Notes)

2 tablespoons light corn syrup

DIRECTIONS:

1 In small bowl over medium saucepan 1/4 full of simmering water melt chocolate.

If you're using white chocolate and want to tint it, stir in a tiny amount of coloring now. You'll have to settle for pastels, since extra dye will seize up the chocolate before you can incorporate the corn syrup and for this mixture you can't use the trick of adding oil to resmooth it.

2 Stir in corn syrup, just barely combining. It will seize up violently; wrap and refrigerate for an hour.

3 Remove chocolate from refrigerator and begin working it with (impeccably clean) hands. Roll out half of the batch at a time to make a 3-inch-by-9-inch strip. If it's sticky, rechill; if it is still sticky, your slab may be too warm. If that is not the case, or if you don't have a marble slab or rolling pin, you may roll out between sheets of plastic wrap, lifting and replacing wrap as chocolate sheet stretches and grows. Chocolate should be no more than 1/8 inch thick.

4 Cut into shapes and press into place.

About Keeping: Will keep for months, wrapped and refrigerated.

Yield: 2 3-inch-by-9-inch strips.

44 *Caramelized Sugar Lattice*

USE FOR:

Layered Custard Cream Parfaits

Poached Pears with Gold Leaves

EQUIPMENT:

1-by-12-by-17-inch sheet pan

Parchment

Measuring spoons

Medium saucepan

Measuring cup

Wooden spoon

Pyrex measuring cup

NOTES:

The dangerous reputation of the process of caramelizing sugar—the basis of so many wonderful confections, used here also in Pistachio Brittle on Chocolate #33—can be daunting. Follow a few simple rules, however, and you will act with the assured finesse of an expert. Remember that the sugar is a molten mass that has gone beyond the boiling point and is therefore much hotter than the water that has boiled away. It is also very sticky. Avoid any skin contact; use only wooden implements that can't conduct the heat to your hand; and don't allow any foreign liquids to splash into the sugar at any time, or it may recrystallize and could spit or boil over. Watch carefully and work quickly once it is ready—when it cools it will be very hard and brittle. Clean utensils by soaking them overnight.

This garnish should not be attempted in very damp weather. The caramelized sugar will absorb the moisture from the air and reliquefy. . . trust me.

INGREDIENTS:

Few drops vegetable oil

2 tablespoons water

1/2 cup sugar

DIRECTIONS:

1 Smear back of sheet pan with vegetable oil, and smooth a pan-sized sheet of parchment onto it.

2 Pour water carefully into bottom of medium saucepan, sprinkle sugar over and allow to absorb without disturbing. Do not get any sugar on the sides of the pan.

3 Bring to a boil over medium heat—do not stir. Continue to cook, watching till all water evaporates and sugar forms large, flat gooey crystals, then turns clear and syrupy before it begins to turn a golden color toward the center. Watch carefully as it colors, stirring with wooden spoon to dissolve any remaining crystals.

When sugar is golden brown remove from heat. It's a good idea to set the pot on a metal, stone or ceramic-tile surface to conduct the intense heat away from the pot. This will slow the cooking more quickly and help prevent the sugar from burning and getting bitter. Allow to sit for 2 minutes.

4 Pour hot caramelized sugar into dry Pyrex measuring cup. (If you don't allow sugar to cool first, the denser shape the sugar assumes in the cup can raise the temperature sufficiently for it to boil out of the cup.) Begin to test the sugar's readiness, pouring a little in a corner of the sheet pan. It should flow in a thin, sticky, glossy stream rather than a sputtery splatter. When it reaches this point, cast a series of parallel lines by moving the stream back and forth across the sheet pan, then cast another series in the opposite direction to form a lattice.

5 Allow to cool, then lift the parchment and peel back to break random shapes for garnish.

About Keeping: If lattice bits are not to be used immediately store in a dry, airtight container—and even by this method do not expect success in very damp weather.

Yield: 1 sheet sugar lattice.

The Desserts

Chevron Strawberries

Stemmed straw-
berries dipped in
white and dark
chocolate.

EQUIPMENT:

2 small bowls

Small saucepan

Whisk

Brush for cleaning
berries

Parchment-lined
sheet pan

Small, heavy-
plastic bag

Rubber spatula

This striking presentation came about as I tried to dress up the huge succulent stemmed strawberries we get in early summer. I combined the two types of coating since they're both so good with the berries and both so good with each other. Served from a buffet or several on a plate as dessert, these strawberries are as well received in the corporate board-rooms of San Francisco as they were at my family reunion barbecue in northern Wisconsin. The simple contrasting squiggle makes a strong graphic statement well worth that third step.

Try to dip these within a few hours of serving. They should be kept in a cool place but preferably not refrigerated, since they tend to sweat when restored to room temperature. The moisture marks the chocolate and loosens the berry, in which case the chocolate stays behind when the fruit is picked up. We wouldn't want that to happen.

The stems make convenient handles, but if only regular, clipped-stem berries are available it has been my experience that people will find a way to convey them to their mouths.

COMPONENTS:

8 ounces white chocolate (more, if dipping bowl is shallow)

8 ounces dark chocolate (more, if dipping bowl is shallow)

20 large, stemmed strawberries

ASSEMBLY:

In a small bowl over saucepan 1/4 full of simmering water melt white chocolate. Whisk to smooth. While chocolate is melting brush berries clean, if necessary. If you must rinse them lay them on towels and make sure they are absolutely dry before you proceed.

Hold strawberry by stem and dip into white chocolate at a 45° angle with the most attractive face of the berry toward you. Watch the progress of the edge of chocolate across the face of the berry until it is halfway up on a diagonal. Lift out of chocolate, shake slightly to remove excess and turn it so the good face points up, then scrape the underside across the edge of the bowl and remove to parch-ment-covered sheet pan. If too much chocolate pools around the base of the berry, you may need to add a few drops of vegetable oil to chocolate to thin it.

When all berries are dipped place them in a cool spot for a few minutes to set the chocolate. In the other small bowl put the dark chocolate over simmering water to melt. Whisk to smooth.

Hold berry with face toward you but at opposite angle from that used the first time. Dip quickly and shake lightly but do not scrape before setting back on sheet pan. When all are done return berries to cool place to set chocolate.

Remelt remaining white chocolate in bowl over pan. Scrape white chocolate into plastic bag, cut small hole at corner and pipe a line across the face of each berry.

About Keeping: Will keep in a cool place a few hours (see Notes).

Serves: 20 dipped strawberries, if good sized and served on plates, serves perhaps 6; more as part of a buffet.

Mexican Chocolate Custard Cake

A dessert halfway between a cake and a custard, served with tropical and other fresh fruit; garnished with whipped cream or crème fraîche and a dash of cinnamon.

EQUIPMENT:
Thin-bladed knife

One of the great disappointments of my earliest travels was the pastry of Spain. Perhaps the result of 700 years of Moorish occupation or, more likely, the lack of dairy farming in this arid land, the offerings were typically huge, greasy, dry and utterly tasteless—a truly alarming set of attributes. Mexico has largely inherited the same lackluster repertoire, except for this inspired creation. It is a contribution to the joys of chocolate that may well cancel all the sins of other Mexican pastries and those of the mother country, too. Halfway between a cake and a pudding, this suspended mass of moist dark chocolate and nuts is also halfway to heaven. A simple slice of this cake is the ideal focus of a composed plate, served with a selection of tropical and other fresh fruit and a dollop of whipped cream or crème fraîche, or set among alternative garnishes as listed below.

COMPONENTS:

1 recipe Chocolate Custard Cake #4

1 recipe Whipped Cream #25 or Whipped Crème Fraîche #26

Dash of cinnamon

2 to 3 papayas, skinned and sliced

2 pints strawberries, brushed or washed and dried

1 large honeydew melon, sliced and rind removed

ASSEMBLY:

Cut cake in 3/4-1-inch slices and lay on plate. Dollop with whipped cream or crème fraîche, dust with cinnamon and surround with prepared fruit.

About Keeping: Once composed serve immediately.

Serves: 10.

Also Try: Garnish with a dollop of Tangerine Curd #22 folded with 1 cup of whipped cream. Cake could also become the center of a formal plate, set in a pool of Vanilla Custard Sauce #31 piped with a zigzag of Bitter Orange Sauce #28, Raspberry Sauce #29 or Apricot Sauce #30. Add a scattering of fresh berries.

Lightning Bolt Dacquoise

Hazelnut meringue layered with coffee buttercream, covered with dark chocolate ganache and tinted, drawn and gilded white chocolate tiles.

EQUIPMENT:
Ruler
Serrated knife
Parchment
12-by-17-inch sheet pan
Piping bag with 2-inch-wide, flat pastry-filling tip
Heavy paper for templates
X-Acto knife

This no-holds-barred showstopper may be too abstract for some—that is, until they taste it. This dacquoise gained its snazzy skin when I realized that the smooth seams chocolate tiles would provide on a cake could make the corny edge piping I hate unnecessary. The designer in me stirred—a chance to ignore entirely the fact that it's a cake!

The first incarnation of this torte was as a Christmas gift box with edible ribbons made as a favor to an old client. At an event in Santa Barbara for First Boston Bank it became a set of 15 cakes in smeared pastels and musical notes atop a chocolate grand piano, reached through a forest of suspended star cookies and chocolate sheet music on stands. More recently I've done a valentine box with hot pink Jim Dine hearts all over it.

I must admit the design here is not for the beginner, but it showcases what beautiful and unique effects can be had with as little as one sheet of chocolate and a little imagination. In any case, it's easier than it looks, and the amazed reactions of guests are a hell of a lot of fun.

NOTES:

Though the whole is complex the 4 parts are relatively easy to make days ahead. The yield is large—you may want to freeze part of the meringue-and-buttercream construction to cover differently another time.

COMPONENTS:

1 recipe Almond-Hazelnut Meringue #5

1 recipe Coffee Buttercream #16

1 recipe Dark Chocolate Ganache #24

1 recipe marbleized white Chocolate Tiles #40(B)

1 recipe tinted Chocolate Tiles #40, one end gilded

ASSEMBLY:

Trim the edges of the meringue layer to a 16-by-11-inch rectangle with a serrated knife. Cut again to make four strips 4 by 11 inches. Lay the strips on parchment on the back of the sheet pan and dry them in a 350°F oven 10 to 15 minutes, till they are crisp but not darkened. Cool completely.

Place 1 strip face down in front of you and pipe on a layer of coffee buttercream. Lay another strip on top, and repeat the sequence till all 4 strips are filled and stacked. You can wrap and refrigerate the dacquoise at this point and prepare your tiles and ganache—or even freeze for a much later completion.

Make a full-scale drawing on heavy paper of your design for the 3 sides of the cake you need to cover, allowing an extra 1/4 inch at the seams for the thickness of the ganache. With the X-Acto knife cut the paper along the lines of your drawing to form patterns for each piece you will need, then cut them out of the appropriate chocolate sheet.

Lay the torte on its side in front of you and pipe on a layer of chocolate ganache, making sure it is cool enough not to run. Apply tiles. Turn it over and cover the other side with ganache and tiles. Finally set it upright and pipe the top with ganache, fitting the top tile pieces to form a flush edge with the sides, and press into place.

About Keeping: If wrapped closely in plastic this torte can be refrigerated, but return it to room temperature before unwrapping or moisture condensation may cause the colors to run. Room temperature is also the ideal for serving since the torte will be easier to cut (use a thin-bladed knife and simply push through) and the flavors will be more accessible. Will keep refrigerated for several days; to keep longer it can be frozen, but don't expect tiles to remain intact.

Serves: 20.

Also Try: Frost with White Chocolate Ganache #23; or use either the white or the Dark Chocolate Ganache #24 with appliqués of Chocolate Decorations #43 instead of chocolate tiles.

Chocolate Tortellini in Pear Broth

Fanned poached pear half with ricotta-and-chestnut-filled chocolate tortellini in reduced Chardonnay and Armagnac pear poaching liquid. Chocolate-dipped anisette *biscotti* on the side.

EQUIPMENT:
Small bowl over small saucepan
Whisk
Parchment-lined sheet pan
Large saucepan
Pasta pot

I had long despaired the wasting of gallons of delicious but useless wine broth in which I've poached pears, and sought a way to salvage it. I had also long considered dessert pasta to be where nouvelle cuisine scrapes bottom—but when it met my poaching liquid, something happened. The bitter chocolate dough with the nutty cheese filling, the hot aromatic pear broth, fruit and crispy cookie together become a dessert far more wonderful than the mere sum of its parts—and a drop-dead visual treat as well.

NOTES:

Poached pears should be made a day or more ahead to allow the flavor of the broth to develop.

COMPONENTS:

4 ounces dark chocolate

12 anisette Italian *biscotti*

Broth and 6 pear halves from 2 recipes Poached Pears #34 (see Notes, above)

1 recipe Chocolate Tortellini #10

2 tablespoons Armagnac or other fine cognac

ASSEMBLY:

In small bowl over saucepan 1/4 full of simmering water, melt chocolate. Whisk to smooth, and dip one end of each of the *biscotti*. Lay *biscotti* on parchment-covered sheet pan and put in cool place to set.

Drain poaching liquid from pears into large saucepan. You will be starting with about 8 cups; reduce this to 6 cups. At full boil this takes 10 to 15 minutes.

In a large pasta pot half full of rapidly boiling water cook Chocolate Tortellini for 3 to 5 minutes—till they are al dente. Drain them, and add to reduced pear broth along with the Armagnac.

Heat soup bowls. Fan-cut 6 pears and lay a pear half at the side of each bowl. Ladle in broth and tortellini. Serve *biscotti* on the side.

About Keeping: Pasta must be cooked close to serving time; the dough will lose its texture if it remains in the broth for long, especially if kept warm.

Serves: 6.

Also Try: Sprinkle with a dusting of Spiced Ground Orange Peel #41.

Chocolate-Pastry-Latticed Apricot Pie

Apricot-almond-brandy filling in a chocolate pastry crust.

EQUIPMENT:
Pastry board
Rolling pin
9-inch pie pan
Pastry wheel
Paring knife

This attractive presentation turns the humble standby pie into a just dessert for a simple meal or a formal one. The chocolate pastry is flexible enough to allow the dense weaving of pastry strips that defines a true lattice-topped pie. Besides their rich color and concentrated flavor, the apricots' texture and density provide a firm base that supports the lattice and allows the pie to hold its shape well when cut. Since apricots' bulk and flavor survive processing they are the only fruit I still buy in cans, one to be enjoyed in winter when fresh choices are limited.

COMPONENTS:

1 recipe Chocolate Pastry Dough #6

1 recipe Apricot Pie Filling #17

1/2 recipe Whipped Cream #25

ASSEMBLY:

Dust pastry board and the first disc of dough with flour, and roll out in a circle. Invert pie pan on top and trim edge to 1-1/2 inches from pan rim. Fold dough in quarters, place in pan and unfold. Add filling. Roll out second disc of dough and cut into 1-inch strips with pastry wheel.

Lay parallel strips 1 inch apart across top of pie; trim ends. Fold alternating strips more than halfway back on themselves, then lay a strip across the center perpendicular to the first set of strips. Flip the folded strips back across the pie, then fold back the alternate strips; lay in each additional strip to the edge of the pie, then from the center to the opposite edge of the pie. Trim ends of all the strips, and fold margin of bottom crust up over them, crimping with your fingers to seal.

Bake at 350°F for 50 minutes or until filling begins to bubble up around the edges. Cool completely before serving. Serve with a dollop of whipped cream.

About Keeping: Can be frozen before being baked. You may hold up to 1 day after baking before serving.

Serves: 8.

Mango and Chocolate Sorbets

Creamy sorbets of mango and chocolate, served with a chocolate-covered spoon; garnished with dark chocolate ribbon.

EQUIPMENT:
Small bowl over small saucepan
6 dessert-service spoons
Parchment-lined sheet pan
Ice cream scoop
6 stemmed glasses or bowls

Colleague and friend Diane Burr, who taught me much about pastry, once said "the raspberry may be the queen of fruit, but mango is the king." Since she is now living out of a hammock on 20 acres of jungle near the Hana coast of Maui, Hawaii—languidly picking her own mangoes, I imagine—she must be a woman who knows what she's talking about. In any case both fruits find their match in chocolate. Here the lush tropical intensity of the mango is complemented by the cool, slightly bitter iciness of chocolate in sorbet form, so unlike chocolate ice cream— it reminds me more of iced Thai coffee. The chocolate-dipped spoon is an accent bound to be remembered.

COMPONENTS:

4 ounces dark chocolate for spoons

1 recipe Chocolate Sorbet #38

1 recipe Mango Sorbet #39

1/2 recipe Chocolate Decorations #43, in dark chocolate

ASSEMBLY:

In small bowl over small saucepan 1/4 full of simmering water, melt chocolate. Dip service spoons in chocolate; to get the drip effect, turn spoon upright in mid drip. Set on parchment-lined pan and put in cool place to set. Refrigerate them briefly, if you will be using them soon.

Scoop sorbets into stemmed glasses or bowls, twist a length of dark chocolate ribbon over the top and serve with chocolate-covered spoon.

About Keeping: Will keep, frozen, indefinitely.

Serves: 6.

Also Try: Both sorbets are also good with Raspberry Sauce #29.

Custard-filled Chocolate Chip Eclairs

Spiral-piped éclairs flecked with chocolate bits, filled with chocolate custard and topped with chocolate-cognac sauce and candied violets.

EQUIPMENT:

1 large piping bag with no tip

The French have long recognized the natural affinity of chocolate for baked doughs, from chocolate croissants to the simple childhood treat of *pain au chocolat*. This pairing of crisp, rich, eggy choux paste with flecks of chocolate brings that happy marriage to the realm of the éclair. My thanks to friend Amy Nathan for its inspiration.

COMPONENTS:

1 recipe Chocolate Chip Eclairs #11

1 recipe Chocolate Custard Filling #20

1/2 recipe Chocolate-Cognac Sauce #27

Candied violets

ASSEMBLY:

Open the pastry lengthwise from the cut edge and remove any doughy membranes that remain inside. Fill piping bag with custard, then fill each éclair. Place an éclair on each plate; pour a stream of chocolate sauce in a zigzag pattern across éclair and out to edge of center of plate. Garnish with candied violets.

This sauce is liquid at slightly warmer than room temperature; if it is the proper consistency it will pour beautifully yet set slightly on the plate and not spread.

About Keeping: Once composed serve immediately.

Serves: 6.

Also Try: This component invites many variations. Substitute Vanilla Custard Filling #19, Whipped Cream #25 or Tangerine Curd #22 folded with 1 cup plain whipped cream. Or use either of the custard fillings lightened as for Layered Custard Cream Parfaits (page 100)—1/2 recipe of the custard folded with 3/4 recipe Whipped Cream #25 (which uses 3/4 cup cream, before whipping, plus the vanilla and cream that suit the custards). Could also be drizzled with Raspberry Sauce #29 rather than Chocolate-Cognac Sauce #27.

Chocolate Chip–Mint Ice Cream Sandwiches

Cakey chocolate cookies filled with homemade chocolate chip–mint ice cream, garnished with fresh mint and served in a cellophane bag.

EQUIPMENT:
Warm serrated knife
4-inch plastic bags and seals

A trompe l'oeil sandwich of ice cream and cookies served in a cellophane bag may at first appear destined for a school lunch pail, then, on second glance, more appropriate to being packed in ice on its way to a family picnic. But the cakey homemade cookies and exquisite homemade chocolate chip–mint ice cream wouldn't be unwelcome on even the most formal plate. In fact, there in particular it might be kind of fun. The ice cream recipe is based on one we made at my grandparents' farm in northern Wisconsin on hot August afternoons. Even with 12 cousins to spell on the crank it seemed to take forever. With the new, freezer-compartment ice cream makers, you don't even have to sweat— and it tastes almost as good.

NOTES:

For this formal presentation I have improved the appearance of a plastic sandwich bag by fastening it with a gold adhesive seal. The stickers avidly collected by children could provide a host of other possibilities.

COMPONENTS:

1 recipe Chocolate Chip–Mint Ice Cream #37

1 recipe Chocolate Sandwich Cookies #7

Fresh mint

ASSEMBLY:

Although homemade ice creams are very dense and usually become much firmer than commercial brands when stored in the freezer, you will still have to work quickly. Loosen ice cream from square plastic containers and cut into 8 1/2-inch to 3/4-inch slices. As you layer each slice between cookies cut the completed sandwich in half diagonally with serrated knife, wrap and store in the freezer. Can be served any time after they have become firm. Garnish with fresh mint sprig.

About Keeping: Cookies can be made several days before assembly; ice cream should be made at least a day ahead to allow to freeze solidly before slicing. If sandwiches are to be kept some time after assembly, tuck each inside an extra, freezer-weight sandwich bag to fight freezer burn.

Serves: 8.

Also Try: Layer the cookies with Mango Sorbet #39, or quarter them and serve at room temperature as a sandwich cookie filled with Coffee Buttercream #16, or Bourbon-Apricot Filling #15.

Bourbon-Apricot Chocolate Torte

Chocolate torte with bourbon-apricot filling, glazed with chocolate ganache and garnished with a molded column.

EQUIPMENT:

Long, thin-bladed serrated knife

Metal tart pan bottom or cardboard

Piping bag fitted with 2-inch-wide filling tip

Metal pastry spatula

This incarnation of the classic "flourless" dark chocolate torte, the same component used in the Chocolate Chocolate Mousse Torte, is close in spirit to the original Viennese Sachertorte. However, replacing the sticky-sweet jam or preserve filling with this chunky, sharp apricot filling achieves a deeply satisfying balance between fruit and chocolate, and one that is accessible all year long. It is simple yet rich and elegant.

NOTES:

A traditional garnish might be a single swirl of icing, a monogram or a fan of chocolate filigree. Here an unusual custom-made mold (I bought it when someone who ordered it failed to return) filled with tinted white chocolate becomes the accent that steals the show, but such an accent could be anything on this sumptuous stage—an off-center row of molded apricot roses or any garnish you choose. (To use a chocolate mold, melt tinted or plain chocolate—see Ingredients Notes—in a bowl over simmering water; fill mold, allow to cool and pop out garnish.)

COMPONENTS:

1 recipe Dark Chocolate Torte #1

1 recipe Bourbon-Apricot Filling #15

1 recipe Dark Chocolate Ganache #24

Any molded white chocolate garnish (or garnish of your choice from Accents and Garnishes section)

ASSEMBLY:

This cake both rises and falls to alarming levels. You did nothing wrong, but you will have to trim the hour-glass-shaped overhang to a smooth edge. Don't waste those tasty scraps! With long serrated knife carefully slice the cake horizontally into two equal layers. Slide tart pan bottom or cardboard into cut, and remove top layer.

Fill piping bag with apricot filling and pipe evenly onto first layer of cake. You may have to pry the tip open a bit to accommodate the chunks of fruit. Slide top layer off its tray onto filling. When ganache is cool enough not to run, frost sides first, with metal pastry spatula. Then scrape remainder of ganache on top, smooth to cover and make a final swirl in a fan pattern. If using molded garnish like the one pictured be sure to emplace it before ganache sets.

About Keeping: Torte will keep up to a week, frosted and refrigerated, though the ganache will lose its luster under refrigeration. Return to room temperature before serving.

For 8 or fewer guests cut the unfrosted torte in half; freeze the other half to frost another time. Can be frozen for several months.

Serves: 16.

Also Try: This could be covered with white Chocolate Tiles #40, much like the Lightning Bolt Dacquoise (page 64), or with White Chocolate Ganache #23.

Raspberries with Custard and Fruit Sauces

A scattering of red and golden raspberries in a pool of custard sauce that's piped with red-raspberry and apricot-sauce squiggles; accented with tinted, striped and zigzagged white chocolate tiles.

EQUIPMENT:

Measuring cup or 2-ounce ladle

2 small, heavy-plastic bags

The place set here may be one of the most fantastic in the book, but it is also one of the simplest: fruit with fruit sauce, custard and chocolate. Rarity is provided by the golden raspberries. If you have never tasted them and have the opportunity, don't pass it up. The experience is of raspberryness magnified—at once sweeter and more piquant. Fragile by nature and with two short seasons in early and late summer, these berries rarely make it to market. When they do, the event is worth celebrating.

NOTES:

For those intimidated by the precision cut of chocolate tiles elsewhere in this book, here's a treatment that can't go wrong.

COMPONENTS:

1 recipe Vanilla Custard Sauce #31

1/2 recipe Raspberry Sauce #29

1/2 recipe Apricot Sauce #30

2 1/2-pint baskets fresh red raspberries

2 1/2-pint baskets fresh golden raspberries, strawberries or blueberries

1 recipe tinted white, striped and zigzagged Chocolate Tiles #40(C)

ASSEMBLY:

Pour about 1/4 cup (2 ounces) custard sauce on each plate, tilting to cover. This will usually be enough to coat the center of a standard, 10-inch dinner plate. Test it. If the custard is too deep, the piped sauce will sink and slip from view.

Put each fruit sauce in its own plastic bag and cut a small hole in the corner. Squirt a squiggle of each across the custard. Scatter with berries and garnish with broken shards of striped and drawn white chocolate tile.

About Keeping: Once composed serve immediately.

Serves: 8.

Also Try: Use strawberries and blueberries with Bitter Orange Sauce #28 instead of apricot sauce. Try other seasonal combinations.

Meringue and Chocolate Checkerboard

Squares of hazelnut meringue covered with dark chocolate ganache and tinted white chocolate tiles in alternating colors; topped with chocolate mousse and tangerine curd, berries and edible blossoms.

EQUIPMENT:
Ruler
Serrated knife
Metal pastry spatula
12-by-17-inch sheet pan
X-Acto knife
2 piping bags with 2-inch-wide, flat filling tip, 1 with star tip for optional garnishes

A dessert buffet can be a sound logistical solution, presented on its own with coffee in a new location, to offer a sweet late in a cocktail hors d'oeuvre party, at a buffet supper or even after a sit-down dinner, when clearing the debris to serve dessert can be daunting. It is also a way of achieving an elaborate display without taking the last-minute time to compose individual plates, and there are many ways to customize it for different effects. Once I even piped these squares with chocolate ganache alphabet letters, rather than this florid display, for Vanna White. As a celebrity hostess hired by Macy's for a benefit celebrating their new food emporium, she was appointed the task of serving dessert—a star attraction all around. Under the direction of Lucinda Young of Edible Art caterers I'd designed a tinted-white-chocolate-tiled Wheel of Fortune, on which Miss White placed the squares to spell the event's theme and which she spun to serve them, looking, I must say, very much at home. Guests thronged the display all evening, but I have a feeling they would have done the same had she been serving Pigs in a Blanket.

COMPONENTS:

1 recipe Almond-Hazelnut Meringue #5

1/2 recipe tinted white Chocolate Tiles #40

1/2 recipe tinted white Chocolate Tiles #40 in contrasting color

1-1/2 recipes Dark Chocolate Ganache #24

1/2 cup Dark Chocolate Mousse #13 (1/10 recipe)

1/2 cup Tangerine Curd #22 (1/4 recipe)

Other garnishes, including edible blossoms, berries, silver ball candies

ASSEMBLY:

Using ruler and serrated knife, trim edges of meringue layer to a 16-by-10-inch rectangle, then score and slice into 2-by-2-inch squares. Place on back of sheet pan and dry in 350°F oven for 10 minutes, till meringue is crisp but not darkened. Cool.

Meanwhile, with ruler and X-Acto knife cut the 2 colors of chocolate tiles in 2-by-2-inch squares. Put chocolate ganache in piping bag fitted with filling tip, and cover several meringue squares at a time with the ganache. Use pastry spatula to separate chocolate tile squares from parchment and place them on ganache—press lightly to secure. Cover half the total number of squares with each color and arrange in a checkerboard design for serving. Pipe with rosettes of mousse and curd, and top with a random selection of garnishes.

About Keeping: The squares can be wrapped and stored a few days but are best enjoyed soon after completion.

Serves: 20 people, 2 squares apiece

Also Try: Vary the combinations of tinted tiles. Pipe with Chocolate Custard Filling #20 or Vanilla Custard Filling #19, or add small scoops of Spiced Mascarpone #14.

Chocolate Chocolate Mousse Torte

Chocolate torte layered with chocolate mousse and fresh raspberries, frosted with whipped cream; served with raspberry sauce.

EQUIPMENT:

Long, thin-bladed serrated knife

Tart-pan bottom or cardboard cake round

Cake plate with 10-inch flat bottom

Rubber spatula

Metal pastry spatula

Plastic wrap

Piping bag with large star tip

This title is more descriptive than redundant—a double dose of dense, moist chocolate torte filled and topped with a slightly creamy yet airy and dry-textured chocolate mousse. The filling layer is studded with raspberries, whose sharp flavor balances well the richness of cake and mousse; the whipped cream around the sides provides the cake a self-contained garnish that lightens the overall effect. In my restaurant experience this torte was the mainstay of my repertoire. It has been as well the choice of a pair of engaged chocaholics for their wedding cake!

COMPONENTS:

1 recipe Dark Chocolate Torte #1

1 recipe Dark Chocolate Mousse #13

2 1/2-pint baskets fresh raspberries

1 recipe Whipped Cream #25

1 recipe Raspberry Sauce #29, optional

ASSEMBLY:

Trim overhanging torte edges and treat yourself to the scraps. With long serrated knife carefully slice the cake horizontally into two equal layers. Because this is essentially a flourless cake there is little gluten to bind it, and it will be crumbly and very delicate. Slide tart pan bottom or cardboard into cut, and lift off the top layer. Slide bottom layer onto cake plate. Any breaks will eventually be cemented by the mousse when it sets.

Before assembly, mousse should be chilled about 2 hours from the time it was made, or till not yet set but no longer runny. With rubber spatula lift half of mousse onto first cake layer. Smooth with metal pastry spatula, taking care to disturb the texture of the mousse as little as possible. Scatter raspberries over the surface, and press in lightly. Invert top cake layer and spread with a small amount of the remaining mousse, flip over onto the raspberries and smooth sides with pastry spatula. Spread rest of mousse on top and smooth with pastry spatula run under hot water. Wrap sides in plastic wrap to retain shape and refrigerate till firm.

Once firm, torte can be wrapped and frozen and will hold for several weeks.

With pastry bag pipe strips of whipped cream from bottom to top all the way around the chilled cake, topping with a row of rosettes around the top edge. Top cake with remaining berries or reserve them for plate garnish. Serve with raspberry sauce, optional.

About Keeping: Refrigerate. Serve within 8 hours once whipped cream is piped.

Serves: 12.

Also Try: This torte will stand on its own merits without raspberries. Try spreading the first layer with Bourbon-Apricot Filling #15 before adding the first layer of mousse, or just use the mousse alone.

Chocolate Crêpes with Flambéed Oranges

Chocolate crêpes filled with fresh orange chunks flambéed in Grand Marnier, topped with whipped cream and spiced ground orange peel.

EQUIPMENT:

Piping bag with 2-inch-wide, flat filling tip

The idea developed here surfaced in the search for a succulent, fruity winter dessert. Even here in the cradle of California cuisine, where there are few weeks in the year when fresh berries aren't available from somewhere on earth, out-of-season fruit is seldom what it should be and can be extremely expensive—while oranges are at their plentiful best. Yet they are rarely used in desserts as themselves. Cut as they are in this dish to minimize tough pulp, and flambéed in liqueur to intensify their flavor, they are quite transformed—the taste is actually akin to that of blueberries. When this dish was served recently to 150 people at a formal sit-down dinner, every plate returned from the dining room scraped clean.

COMPONENTS:

1 recipe Flambéed Oranges #18

1 recipe Chocolate Crêpes #12

1 recipe Whipped Cream #25

1 recipe Spiced Ground Orange Peel #41

ASSEMBLY:

Place approximately 1/4 cup flambéed oranges in the center of the lower 2/3 of a crêpe. Fold the upper edge 1/3 down over the oranges, then fold in each side so it becomes an envelope with the open flap toward you, spilling oranges.

Place 2 composed crêpes on each plate. Garnish with 3 folds of whipped cream piped with the wide, flat filling tip and a sprinkling of ground orange peel.

About Keeping: Serve immediately.

Serves: 6.

Also Try: Spread a tablespoon or 2 of Spiced Mascarpone #14 onto the crêpe under the oranges before you fill it. Could also replace whipped cream with Whipped Crème Fraîche #26.

Chocolate Ribbon Cake

Chocolate génoise layered with chocolate custard and nectarines, frosted with white chocolate ganache and pastel chocolate decorations.

EQUIPMENT:
Parchment
Ruler
Serrated knife
Plastic wrap
Piping bag with 2-inch-wide, flat filling tip
Metal pastry spatula

This outrageous presentation—a showcase for the potential of chocolate decorations—cloaks my most basic cake, which is just as good, believe it or not, without its finery. A simple chocolate sponge cake and chocolate custard filling can be paired with a full cavalcade of peak-season fruit all summer long; in this case, nectarines. The chocolate decorations are a flexible medium that opens a realm of possibilities completely different from that of the chocolate tiles and can have enormous impact. A La Jolla matron who'd once seen this cake at a dessert tasting for a charity ball identified me with it in an unrelated encounter—3 years later.

NOTES:

The three mixtures used here may take time, but they last refrigerated for months. And making the cutouts, once you get to it, is more purely child's play than any other form of expression in the discipline.

In this assembly 1 of the 4 strips of génoise will be left over. Well, nobody's perfect. Actually I've found that a bit extra of something is extremely useful in the making of single whole desserts like this, which offer absolutely no way to snitch a bit before serving; the excess will help keep impatient hands from carving bits off the Masterpiece till the guests are served.

Your use of decorations may make the cake difficult to cut; in this case remove sections of the design to garnish the plates as you serve.

COMPONENTS:

1 recipe Chocolate Génoise #3

1 recipe Chocolate Custard Filling #20

3 to 4 nectarines, peeled and sliced

1 recipe White Chocolate Ganache #23

3 recipes Chocolate Decorations #43

ASSEMBLY:

Flip génoise onto parchment on work surface. Working with ruler and serrated knife trim edges to form a 16-by-11-inch rectangle. Cut into 4 strips 4 by 11 inches each.

Lay 1 strip on serving tray. If you want to avoid cleaning areas around cake later, cover them with plastic wrap. Fill piping bag fitted with 2-inch-wide filling tip with chocolate custard, and pipe a layer onto the cake. Lay on nectarine slices end to end lengthwise, so you will cut across them when slicing. Pipe a thin layer of custard on the next cake strip and flip it over on top of the nectarines. Repeat. Wrap cake tightly with plastic wrap and refrigerate for a few hours or up to 1 day before proceeding. During this time, prepare the chocolate decorations, 1 batch in each of 3 colors, and white chocolate ganache.

If ganache has been made in advance and remelted, it may need to be refrigerated again to reach proper piping texture. When it is ready, fill cleaned and dried piping bag, again fitted with the 2-inch-wide filling tip, and cover cake, sides and top; smooth with pastry spatula run under hot water.

Work, roll and cut chocolate decorations as explained in recipe #43. Press decorations into place. To simplify slicing, remove sections of ribbon as you cut and add to plates as served.

About Keeping: Keep cake in a cool place till serving. Although many of the elements are forgiving while unassembled, the finished cake should be eaten within a few hours of completion.

Serves: 14.

Also Try: Fill with Vanilla Custard Filling #19 and other fruit or even with Spiced Mascarpone #14. Frost by piping with Whipped Cream #25 or Whipped Crème Fraîche #26.

Mocha Mousse with Bitter Orange Sauce

Mocha and vanilla custard cream mousses layered in a mold; served with bitter orange sauce.

EQUIPMENT:

Bowl of hot water for loosening mousse from mold

This was a case where the mold came first, then the molded. Photographer Patricia Brabant found this especially fine and unusual antique crockery mold, which led me to find a use for it. I was already well out of my Jell-O phase but have always loved the drama of a molded dessert. The separation of leaf and flower inspired this two-toned beauty, a dense Bavarian-style jelled mocha mousse and matching layer of vanilla cream meant to melt in the mouth while the essences of coffee, chocolate, cream and orange marry.

NOTES:

Never having used a crockery mold before, I was surprised to find I prefer it to metal. Since its absorption of heat is more subtle, or perhaps because of a slicker surface, it releases the filling more easily with detail intact and a minimum of hot-water dunking.

COMPONENTS:

1 recipe Molded Mocha and Cream Mousse #35

1 recipe Bitter Orange Sauce #28

ASSEMBLY:

Dip set mold in hot water to loosen contents. Invert onto serving plate and unmold; you may have to pull at the edge to free mousse from the vacuum. Surround with bitter orange sauce.

About Keeping: Will keep, refrigerated, several days before unmolding.

Serves: 6.

Also Try: Use individual molds or custard cups. Also excellent served with Raspberry Sauce #29.

Fruit and Cream with Chocolate Triangles

Tinted, dark-spattered white chocolate triangles and whipped crème fraîche; with strawberries, kiwi and cantaloupe cubes in Midori, garnished with a chiffonade of fresh mint.

EQUIPMENT:
Ruler
X-Acto knife
Paring knife

When I first began experimenting with white chocolate sheets I was intrigued by the idea of using them to create a 3-dimensional effect by standing them up. Then caterer John Baylin in San Diego delivered the challenge of creating a dessert for his first major sit-down dinner—a light spring meal at the La Jolla Museum of Contemporary Art for 70 people. This was the result—a simple plate of fruit and cream updated. The sweet white chocolate is countered by the sour cast of whipped crème fraîche. Only the melon is treated, here—cut in cubes (so they wouldn't roll on the plate!), soaked in Midori (melon liqueur) and garnished with finely sliced fresh mint leaves.

COMPONENTS:

1 recipe tinted white Chocolate Tiles with dark chocolate drizzle #40(A)

1 recipe Whipped Crème Fraîche #26

1 pint strawberries, brushed or, if necessary, rinsed and thoroughly dried

3 kiwis, skinned and sliced

Cubes cut from 1 cantaloupe, doused with Midori liqueur

Mint leaves cut in very thin strips

ASSEMBLY:

With ruler and X-Acto knife cut chocolate-tile sheet into triangles measured to fit your plates.

Spoon a dollop of whipped crème fraîche in the center of each plate and push three chocolate triangles into each from the side, so they stand. Scatter fruit between them and garnish melon with mint.

About Keeping: Once assembled serve immediately.

Serves: 6.

Also Try: Any complementary combination of fresh seasonal fruit.

The Tomlin Tart

Individual chocolate pastry shells filled with vanilla custard, topped with fresh fig, kiwi and papaya and glazed with apple jelly.

EQUIPMENT:
Fork
Paring knife
Small melon baller
Small saucepan
Small pastry brush

While visiting friends once in Los Angeles I happened to renew contact with a woman I had met years before at an art fair in Italy, Cheryl Swannack. She had since begun working for Lily Tomlin and eventually became her stage manager. Over lunch at Musso & Frank's Grill in Hollywood I told her of the new focus of my work being food, and she mentioned needing a chef to cook for the writers and household during the production of Lily's next TV special. At the time Lily had just completed a 3-year refurbishment of the old W.C. Fields mansion, in the Los Feliz area, and was ready for professional staff. It was decided that I would "audition" by preparing some special dish—but what? Since I was leaving the next day and had to deliver before Lily went out that evening, I had one afternoon. Desserts were already my forte then, but the place I was staying was ill-equipped to produce what I was used to. There was, however, a backyard fig tree heavily laden with perfect ripe fruit. This fresh fruit tart was the result. Despite great difficulty finding the house, including a run-in with LA police, I arrived in time for introductions but not for tasting. On return to San Francisco the next evening I got a phone call—I had the job!

COMPONENTS:

1/2 recipe Chocolate Pastry Dough #6

1/2 recipe Vanilla Custard Filling #19

6 figs, washed and dried

3 kiwis, skinned and sliced

1 papaya

1/2 cup apple jelly for glaze

ASSEMBLY:

Press pastry into 8 3-inch individual tart pans, prick bottoms with fork and bake at 350°F for 20 minutes. Remove from pans to cool. Fill with custard. Cut figs into quarters and place 3 back to back on each center to form a pyramid. Surround with half-slices of kiwi and small scoops of papaya cut with the melon baller. Melt apple jelly in saucepan and brush on fruit to glaze.

About Keeping: Will keep only a few hours after assembly.

Serves: 8.

Also Try: Since fresh figs are difficult to find in much of the country, top with any variety and many combinations of fresh or even poached, well-drained fruit.

Layered Chocolate Angel Food Cake

Chocolate angel food cake filled with layers of tangerine curd, frosted with whipped crème fraîche and marbleized white chocolate shards.

EQUIPMENT:

Long, thin-bladed serrated knife

2 piping bags; 1 fitted with 2-inch-wide filling tip, the second with small leaf tip

Metal pastry spatula

When I first gave a recipe for lemon curd to my mother, she layered it into an angel food cake to serve at a church luncheon. There is an economy of means here; you get a striking, cloud-high layer cake without making three separate pans of batter. Also, citrus is a traditionally appropriate complement to this kind of cake. With vast quantities of vagrant egg whites in my life—a result of much custard making—I decided to reassess this American classic for myself. I had forgotten the endearing texture of angel food, and in testing this interpretation I reminded many others of its charm as well. With the icing treatment here it would make a wonderful birthday or special-occasion cake, served with a scoop of your favorite ice cream.

COMPONENTS:

1 recipe Chocolate Angel Food Cake #2

1 recipe Tangerine Curd #22

2 recipes Whipped Crème Fraîche #26

1 recipe marbleized, tinted white Chocolate Tiles #40(B)

ASSEMBLY:

With long serrated knife slice cake horizontally into 3 equal layers. Put tangerine curd in piping bag with filling tip, and pipe half of it evenly onto top of first layer. Replace second layer and repeat. Top with third layer.

With metal pastry spatula spread top and sides of cake with whipped crème fraîche. Break chocolate tile into random shapes and stick to frosted surfaces.

In second pastry bag with leaf tip pipe the rest of the whipped crème fraîche back and forth between the tiles of chocolate all over the cake.

About Keeping: Will keep up to 2 days before frosting, refrigerated.

Serves: 12.

Also Try: Fill cake with Spiced Mascarpone #14 or Bourbon-Apricot Filling #15. Instead of frosting it try a simple drizzle of White or Dark Chocolate Ganache #23 or #24.

Chocolate-Hazelnut Pie

Chocolate pastry shell with chocolate-hazelnut pie filling, garnished with a piped whipped cream bow.

EQUIPMENT:
Rolling pin
Pastry board
1 9-inch pie pan
Piping bag and 1-inch flat tip

Nut pies have always seemed to me to be the dessert easiest to have too much of. I used to reserve having them for the final indulgent insult to an all-out pig-out at some crudely seductive barbecued-rib joint. The first great hazelnut pie I encountered was made by a one-time pastry chef at the Station House Cafe in Point Reyes Station, California, long known for its great food and terrible attitude. When even scheduling my visits to coincide with this baker's weekly shift failed to deliver my quarry, I knew I had to create my own. The addition of bitter chocolate cuts the sweetness of what is essentially a sugar custard underlying the nuts, ameliorating the classic chess, molasses or sugar pie that all but Southerners love to hate.

COMPONENTS:

1/2 recipe Chocolate Pastry Dough #6

1 recipe Chocolate-Hazelnut Pie Filling #21

1/2 recipe Whipped Cream #25

ASSEMBLY:

Roll out dough on lightly floured board in a circle, place pie pan top down on it and trim excess dough to 2 inches from edge of pan. Fold dough in quarters and unfold in pan, tucking the margin under itself and crimping with your fingers. Refrigerate shell and preheat oven to 400°F.

Prebake shell for 10 minutes. Fill shell with hazelnut pie filling and return to oven. Bake for 15 minutes at 400°F, then reduce heat to 350° without opening door and bake another 30 minutes, till edges of filling begin to rise and center is set. Allow to cool before serving.

Pipe a whipped cream bow on each slice, as pictured, or simply dollop each plate with cream on the side.

About Keeping: Serve fresh. Leftovers will keep a couple of days.

Serves: 8.

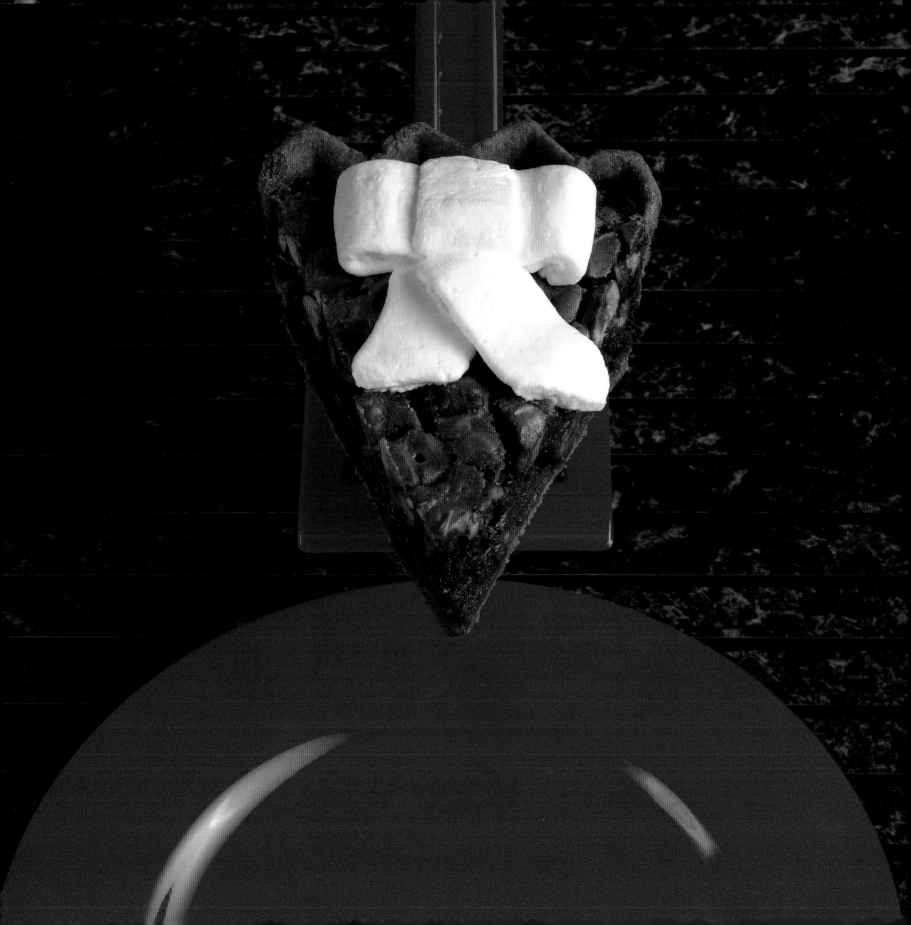

Poached Pears with Gold Leaves

Poached pear halves filled with spiced Mascarpone in a pool of custard sauce and bitter orange sauce, garnished with caramelized sugar lattice, gilded white chocolate leaves and spiced ground orange peel.

EQUIPMENT:
X-Acto knife
Cardboard for leaf template
Measuring cup or 2-ounce ladle
Paring knife
Soup spoon or small ice cream scoop
Small, heavy-plastic bag

This elegant dessert evolved in collaboration with Lucinda Young of Edible Art, when the company presented a special birthday dinner for the owner of a luxury car dealership. Since he had recently completed construction of a sleek, beautifully detailed sales and service center, the dinner was served there at tables scattered among the gleaming Jaguars and Mercedes. All creamy pale and tawny gold, the dessert is a showy and complex display, yet its elements are simple and most can be made days ahead of serving.

COMPONENTS:

1 recipe gilded white Chocolate Tiles #40(E)

1 recipe Vanilla Custard Sauce #31

1 recipe Poached Pears #34

1 recipe Spiced Mascarpone #14

1 recipe Bitter Orange Sauce #28

1 recipe Caramelized Sugar Lattice #44

1 recipe Spiced Ground Orange Peel #41

ASSEMBLY:

With X-Acto knife cut leaf shape from cardboard. Lay it on gilded chocolate sheet and use same blade to cut 12 leaf shapes from chocolate.

With measuring cup or ladle pour 1/4 cup of custard sauce onto each of 6 large dinner plates, tilting each to cover the bottom. Cut a small slice off the bottom of 6 pear halves so they won't roll, and scoop 1/4 cup of the Mascarpone into each hollow. Set them in the sauce in the upper half of each plate.

Cut 3 of the best remaining pear halves in half again, and slice each half nearly through 4 times to fan; spread and lay on plate from the filled half to over the lower rim of the plate.

Drizzle the bitter orange sauce from a heavy-plastic bag with a small hole cut in the corner into the custard around the pears.

Break the sheet of sugar lattice into shards and press one into each scoop of Mascarpone. Sprinkle spiced orange peel over the whole plate, and lay a gilded chocolate leaf on either side of fanned pear.

About Keeping: Once assembled do not attempt to keep.

Serves: 6.

Also Try: This composition can be altered in perhaps more ways than any other included here—to range from dreamy to brightly colored and playful. The pear can be filled with Vanilla Custard Filling #19, Chocolate Custard Filling #20, or Whipped Crème Fraîche #26. Raspberry Sauce #29 or Chocolate-Cognac Sauce #27 can be piped into the custard pool. The chocolate leaves can be replaced with any kind of white Chocolate Tiles #40. The sugar lattice can be omitted or be replaced with Chocolate Filigree #42.

Layered Custard Cream Parfaits

Vanilla and chocolate custards folded into whipped cream and layered, with fresh raspberries; garnished with an array of whimsical accents.

EQUIPMENT:

3 large piping bags, one with large star tip

2 small bowls

Wire whisk

Rubber spatula

6 parfait or wine glasses

There is something intrinsically spectacular about layers of filling as seen through the side of a glass, and yet few effects are so easy to achieve. The challenge that caused the creation of this dessert was a major museum fundraising event for 700 guests. While there was a need to match the special qualities of the institution with a really glamorous display, budget restrictions excluded the expensive ingredients and work-intensive nature of the most obvious choices. In this case whipped cream was folded into custard filling to lighten it, then combined with raspberries and a whimsical accent. The prefilled rented glasses went to the party in their own crates, and in the end not one guest could resist the temptation of that last berry.

COMPONENTS:

1-1/2 recipes Whipped Cream #25

1/2 recipe Vanilla Custard Filling #19

1/2 recipe Chocolate Custard Filling #20

2 1/2-pint baskets fresh raspberries

1 recipe any Chocolate Tiles #40, Caramelized Sugar Lattice #44, Chocolate Filigree #42 or Chocolate Decorations #43

ASSEMBLY:

Reserve about 1-1/2 cups of the whipped cream in the piping bag with the large star tip, and refrigerate.

Scrape each custard into a small bowl; add 1/2 cup whipped cream to each and whisk it in, smoothing texture. Divide the rest of the cream between the custards, and fold in gently with the rubber spatula.

Place a few berries in the bottom of each glass. Fill the 2 remaining piping bags with the 2 custard mixtures; pipe 1 layer of each alternately into the glasses, always against the glass first—in a ring, watching and turning the glass as you go—then filling in the center of that layer. Top the glass with a layer of more berries, a coiled turban of piped whipped cream and your chosen garnish.

About Keeping: Will keep 1 day covered, without whipped cream and garnish.

Serves: 6.

Also Try: If you've got a little more time and a steady hand, try piping a thin ring of Raspberry Sauce #29 against the glass between each layer of custard.

Joan Collins' Broken Heart

Coeur à la crème with a crack that's lined in dark chocolate tiles; served with raspberry sauce.

EQUIPMENT:
Double thickness of cheesecloth to line mold
1-quart heart-shaped mold with drainage holes
X-Acto knife
Ruler
Large piping bag without tip
Metal rack set over pan

I have loved the French dessert coeur à la crème from the time I first discovered it—the traditional heart-shaped mold and also the texture, best described as that of a cream cheese mousse. The process that produces it is unusual and interesting to observe but very simple. Cream and cottage cheeses are combined with whipped cream and used to fill a cheesecloth-lined mold with holes in the bottom through which the whey remaining in the cheese seeps out, firming the mixture inside. Thus the heart shape is a pun on the process—only the "hearts" of the cheeses remain, as the name states.

Asked to create a dessert for a small buffet dinner for the cast of "Dynasty," I was struck that the marital Sturm und Drang of the series could be well served by taking the pun one step further. I would make a broken heart, from whose dark-chocolate-sheathed break spills a blood-red raspberry sauce.

I had just laid the heart's tray on the buffet as Joan Collins entered, spied it and caught her breath.

"Oh! Someone really made this?"

"Just for you, Joan," I said from behind her as she turned and I presented myself.

"It's absolutely marvelous," she enthused—as will you.

NOTES:

This version is particularly well flavored and doesn't really need fresh fruit, a usual accompaniment. The light, fluffy liqueured mousse is wonderful against the cold, crisp bitter-chocolate tiles and fruity raspberry sauce. If you don't have a regulation coeur à la crème mold buy a throwaway aluminum cake pan, punch holes in a heart-shaped pan you seldom use or rig a temporary structure with foil shaped over cardboard.

COMPONENTS:

1 recipe Coeur à la Crème Mixture #36

1/2 recipe dark Chocolate Tiles #40

1 recipe Raspberry Sauce #29

ASSEMBLY:

Wet the cheesecloth, squeeze out excess moisture and line the mold.

With X-Acto knife cut 2 strips of chocolate tile of width equal to the depth of the mold, the length several inches longer than the diameter of the mold. Cut both strips again into 3 unequal lengths and place them, in matching pairs, on top of each other.

Fill the piping bag with coeur à la crème mixture. (A large paper clip will keep the filling from pouring through before you're ready.) Test standing the tiles in the mold to figure where your heart will break, making sure to keep them and your hands cold. Remove the tiles, and pipe a small amount of the mixture in a line where the pairs of tiles will be. Push the tiles into the mixture so they will

stand, their lengths flush. Pipe remaining amount alternately on either side of crack, and fold excess cheesecloth over filled mold. Place mold on metal rack over pan to drain, and refrigerate at least 24 hours or up to 2 days.

To unmold, peel back cheesecloth from the surface, invert a plate over the top and turn both over. Remove mold and cheesecloth and, slipping a knife into the crack between the pairs of tiles, scoot the 2 halves apart to open the break. Pour raspberry sauce into break and pool it around the heart; serve more on the side in a pitcher.

About Keeping: Can be made up to 2 days before serving.

Serves: 4 to 6.

Also Try: Line crack with plain white Chocolate Tiles #40; serve with Bitter Orange Sauce #28, Apricot Sauce #30 or even Chocolate-Cognac Sauce #27.

Assorted Cookies and Sweets

On a dessert buffet, packaged for gifts or just to munch on, these little sweets will please the eye as well as the palate. The techniques for producing them vary widely. Full recipes for three of those that are easiest to produce appear in the next few pages.

Bourbon Prunes in Chocolate #32 will surprise many diners. Although prunes have a terrible reputation in this country they are widely used in Europe, successfully paired with everything from pastry to wild game. Glazed with bourbon sugar and dipped in milk chocolate they are truly wonderful.

Baby Carrots in White Chocolate may seem strange but make more sense when you taste them; there's an allusion here to the classic carrot cake with its sweet white icing, and the 2 textures offer a pleasing resonance of crispness. They were born as a garnish for a special cake I once did—a dacquoise covered in faux-wood-grained chocolate sheets to look like a cutting board, complete with gray chocolate knives with meringue handles. The event was a symposium on ritual and food attended by, of all people, Jesuits and psychologists. They were good enough together to survive their one-night stand. The carrots and chocolate, that is . . .

EQUIPMENT:
Small bowl over medium saucepan
Whisk
Parchment-lined sheet pan

COMPONENTS:

8 ounces white chocolate

1 bunch baby carrots (about 20)

ASSEMBLY:

Melt chocolate in small bowl over saucepan 1/4 full of simmering water. Whisk to smooth. Trim carrot tops about 3 inches from stem at a 45° angle, wash carrots (but don't scrub; leave skin intact to avoid carrot's moisture meeting chocolate) and dry thoroughly. Dip carrots in chocolate, raking the underside of each on edge of bowl as you remove it. Lay them on parchment-lined sheet pan till chocolate is set.

Crystallized Ginger in Semisweet Chocolate combines the tastes of ginger and chocolate that for many of my Jewish friends is a fond childhood memory. For those who've grown to love the zing of ginger this is the ultimate treatment.

EQUIPMENT:
Small bowl over medium saucepan
Whisk
Parchment-lined sheet pan

COMPONENTS:

4 ounces semisweet chocolate

3 ounces crystallized ginger

ASSEMBLY:

Melt chocolate in a small bowl over small saucepan 1/4 full of simmering water. Whisk to smooth.

Dip 3/4 of each slice of ginger into the chocolate, then lay on parchment-lined sheet pan. Put in a cool, dry place to set.

Chocolate-Hazelnut Shortbread Squares contain the same filling found in the Chocolate-Hazelnut Pie, baked atop a chocolate version of classic Scottish shortbread.

COMPONENTS:

1 recipe Chocolate Shortbread #9

1 recipe Chocolate-Hazelnut Pie Filling #21

ASSEMBLY:

Bake the pan of chocolate shortbread for 20 minutes at 350°F. While shortbread is baking, make the pie filling.

Stir the hazelnut mixture well and pour over the shortbread, taking care to distribute the nuts evenly. Return to oven and bake another 30 to 35 minutes, till topping is set. Cool and cut into 32 squares.

Rich Hot Chocolate is a "kids of all ages" pleaser that recollects the comforts of childhood yet panders to an adult palate, with a creamy base and a hint of spice. It is substantial enough to be served in demitasse cups with a dessert buffet.

EQUIPMENT:
Can opener
Large saucepan
Measuring spoons
Wooden spoon
Whisk
Measuring cup

COMPONENTS:

10 ounces dark chocolate

1 12-ounce can evaporated milk

1 tablespoon good-quality instant coffee granules

1 stick cinnamon

3-1/2 cups milk

ASSEMBLY:

In saucepan over low heat melt chocolate together with evaporated milk, instant coffee and cinnamon, stirring occasionally with wooden spoon.

When chocolate is completely melted whisk mixture to smooth. Whisk in the milk and heat through.

Pistachio Brittle on Chocolate #33 features the nuts often used as a garnish because of their unusual green color. This presentation showcases their unique flavor.

Striped Refrigerator Cookies #8 are a variation on the classic pinwheel cookie, but they're actually easier to accurately form. The dough can be kept refrigerated for several weeks; you may wish to slice and bake a few at a time so they're always fresh.

About Keeping: The cookies will stay fresh several days. Candies once dipped should be served within a day to prevent problems with untempered chocolate (see Technique Notes). Carrots must be served soon after dipping to retain crispness; if necessary, they will last 2 or 3 hours refrigerated. (Any bloom that develops in the refrigerator will not show on untinted white chocolate of either type.) The hot chocolate will last for up to a week, refrigerated.

Serves: Since the cookie recipes yield 32 cookies each, the candies, including carrots, approximately 20 each, and the hot chocolate fills approximately 24 demitasse cups, this total buffet could serve between 20 and 30 guests.

Indexes